UNDER THE SEA

How to Use Your SD-X Reader with This Book

This highly informative book introduces you and your child to aquatic life in a new interactive format. You can read the book and study the rich illustrations, but a touch of the SD-X Reader adds in-depth audio information, word definitions, and learning games to the pictures and text.

1. Press the Power button to turn the SD-X Reader on or off. The LED will light up when the SD-X Reader is on.

2. Touch the volume buttons found on this page or on the Table of Contents page in this book to adjust the volume.

3. Throughout the book, words in this color provide additional information when they're touched with the SD-X Reader. Objects on the page may also play additional audio.

4. At the top left corner of each spread, you'll see circles like these: ● ● Touch a circle to start a learning game or quiz. Touch the same circle again to stop playing the game. Touch another circle to start another learning game or quiz.

5. Some learning games will ask you to use Ⓣ Ⓕ buttons or Ⓐ Ⓑ buttons to answer. For other learning games, touch objects on the page to answer.

6. When you've answered all the questions in a learning game, you'll hear your score.

7. After two minutes of inactivity, the SD-X Reader will beep and go to sleep.

8. If the batteries are low, the SD-X Reader will beep twice and the LED will start blinking. Replace the batteries by following the instructions on the next page. The SD-X Reader uses two AAA batteries.

9. To use headphones or earbuds, plug them into the headphone jack on the bottom of the SD-X Reader.

CHANGE THE VOLUME WITH THESE BUTTONS:

▲ ▼

UP   DOWN

Battery Information
Includes two replaceable AAA batteries (UM-4 or LR03).

Battery Installation
1. Open battery door with small screwdriver.
2. Install new batteries according to +/- polarity. If batteries are not installed properly, the device will not function.
3. Replace battery door; secure with small screw.

Battery Safety
Batteries must be replaced by adults only. Properly dispose of used batteries. See battery manufacturer for disposal recommendations. Do not mix alkaline, standard (carbon-zinc), or rechargeable (nickel-cadmium) batteries. Do not mix old and new batteries. Only recommended batteries of the same or equivalent type should be used. Remove weakened or dead batteries. Never short-circuit the supply terminals. Non-rechargeable batteries are not to be recharged. Do not use rechargeable batteries. If batteries are swallowed, in the USA, promptly see a doctor and have the doctor phone 1-202-625-3333 collect. In other countries, have the doctor call your local poison control center. This product uses 2 AAA batteries (2 X 1.5V = 3.0 V). Use batteries of the same or equivalent type as recommended. The supply terminals are not to be short-circuited. Batteries should be changed when sounds mix, distort, or become otherwise unintelligible as batteries weaken. The electrostatic discharge may interfere with the sound module. If this occurs, please simply restart the sound module by pressing any key.

In Europe, the dustbin symbol indicates that batteries, rechargeable batteries, button cells, battery packs, and similar materials must not be discarded in household waste. Batteries containing hazardous substances are harmful to the environment and to health. Please help to protect the environment from health risks by telling your children to dispose of batteries properly and by taking batteries to local collection points. Batteries handled in this manner are safely recycled.

Warning: Changes or modifications to this unit not expressly approved by the party responsible for compliance could void the user's authority to operate the equipment.

NOTE: This equipment has been tested and found to comply with the limits for a Class B digital device, pursuant to Part 15 of the FCC Rules. These limits are designed to provide reasonable protection against harmful interference in a residential installation. This equipment generates, uses, and can radiate radio frequency energy and, if not installed and used in accordance with the instructions, may cause harmful interference to radio communications. However, there is no guarantee that interference will not occur in a particular installation. If this equipment does cause harmful interference to radio or television reception, which can be determined by turning the equipment off and on, the user is encouraged to try to correct the interference by one or more of the following measures: Reorient or relocate the receiving antenna. Increase the separation between the equipment and receiver. Connect the equipment into an outlet on a circuit different from that to which the receiver is connected. Consult the dealer or an experienced radio TV technician for help.

Published by Louis Weber, C.E.O., Publications International, Ltd.
7373 North Cicero Avenue
Lincolnwood, Illinois 60712

Ground Floor, 59 Gloucester Place
London W1U 8JJ

Customer Service: 1-888-724-0144 or Customer_Service@pubint.com

www.pilbooks.com

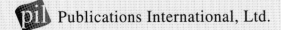 Publications International, Ltd.

Manufactured in China.

8 7 6 5 4 3 2 1

ISBN-10: 1-60553-919-8
ISBN-13: 978-1-60553-919-5

CONTENTS

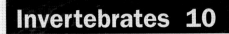
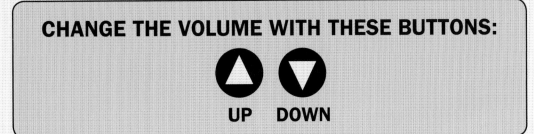

CHANGE THE VOLUME WITH THESE BUTTONS:

▲   ▼

UP   DOWN

Traces of Ancient Life

Millions of years ago, our planet was not as we know it today. The continents were arranged differently, and the climate, flora, and fauna were different. How do we know this? We have learned these things by finding and studying *fossils*, remains of past life-forms that are preserved in both geography and time. The Ediacara, in southern Australia, and the Burgess Shale, in Canada, are two regions with extensive fossil beds of soft-bodied *invertebrates*. Both areas have shed light on what is known as the Cambrian explosion.

Burgess Shale

CANADA
Latitude 51° 25' 30" N
Longitude 116° 30' 00" W

This fossil bed is outstanding for the variety of creatures found.

DICKINSONIA *SPECIES*

Ediacara

AUSTRALIA
Latitude 35° 15' S
Longitude 149° 28' E

The first specimens were found in the Ediacara Hills.

600 million years

AGE OF THE FIRST SPECIMENS FOUND

CHARNIA

JELLYFISH
Ediacaran

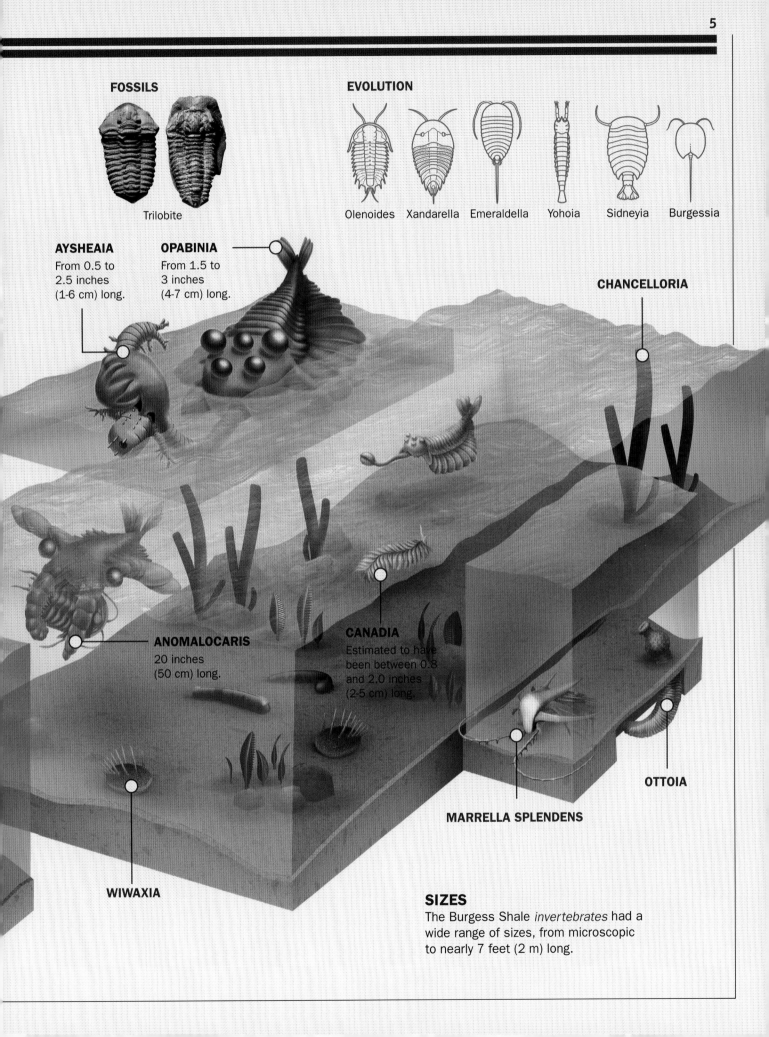

FOSSILS

Trilobite

EVOLUTION

Olenoides Xandarella Emeraldella Yohoia Sidneyia Burgessia

AYSHEAIA
From 0.5 to
2.5 inches
(1-6 cm) long.

OPABINIA
From 1.5 to
3 inches
(4-7 cm) long.

CHANCELLORIA

ANOMALOCARIS
20 inches
(50 cm) long.

CANADIA
Estimated to have
been between 0.8
and 2.0 inches
(2-5 cm) long.

MARRELLA SPLENDENS

OTTOIA

WIWAXIA

SIZES
The Burgess Shale *invertebrates* had a
wide range of sizes, from microscopic
to nearly 7 feet (2 m) long.

Terrestrial and Marine Algae

As long as there is water, the survival of an alga is assured. *Algae* are found both in the oceans and in freshwater, but not all can survive in both environments. Depth, temperature, and salt concentrations of water are characteristics that determine whether algae can live in a given area. Algae can be green, brown, or red. Of the three, red algae are found in the deepest waters. Some *species* of algae can live outside of water, but they are nevertheless found in humid places, such as in mud or on stone walls or rocks.

◀ FUCUS

◀ PORPHYRA

◀ ULVA

▲ MACROCYSTIS

Light

As depth increases, water absorbs sunlight and produces a loss in color.

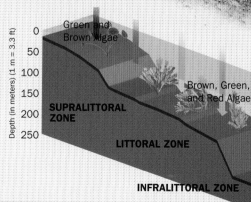

Depth (in meters) (1 m = 3.3 ft)

0 — Green and Brown Algae
50
100
150 — Brown, Green, and Red Algae
200
250

SUPRALITTORAL ZONE

LITTORAL ZONE

INFRALITTORAL ZONE

Red Algae

7,000

SPECIES OF GREEN *ALGAE*

❶ Depth

MARINE WATER

FRESHWATER

❷ Concentration of Salts

Salts	%
HCO$_3^-$	0.4
Ca^{2+}	1.2
Mg^{2+}	3.7
Na$^+$	30.6
K$^+$	1.1
Cl$^-$	55.1
SO$_4^{2-}$	7.7

Salts	%
Ca^{2+}	17
Mg^{2+}	3.4
Na$^+$	3.0
K$^+$	1.8
Cl$^-$	3.3
SO$_4^{2-}$	8.2
HCO$_3^-$	63.5

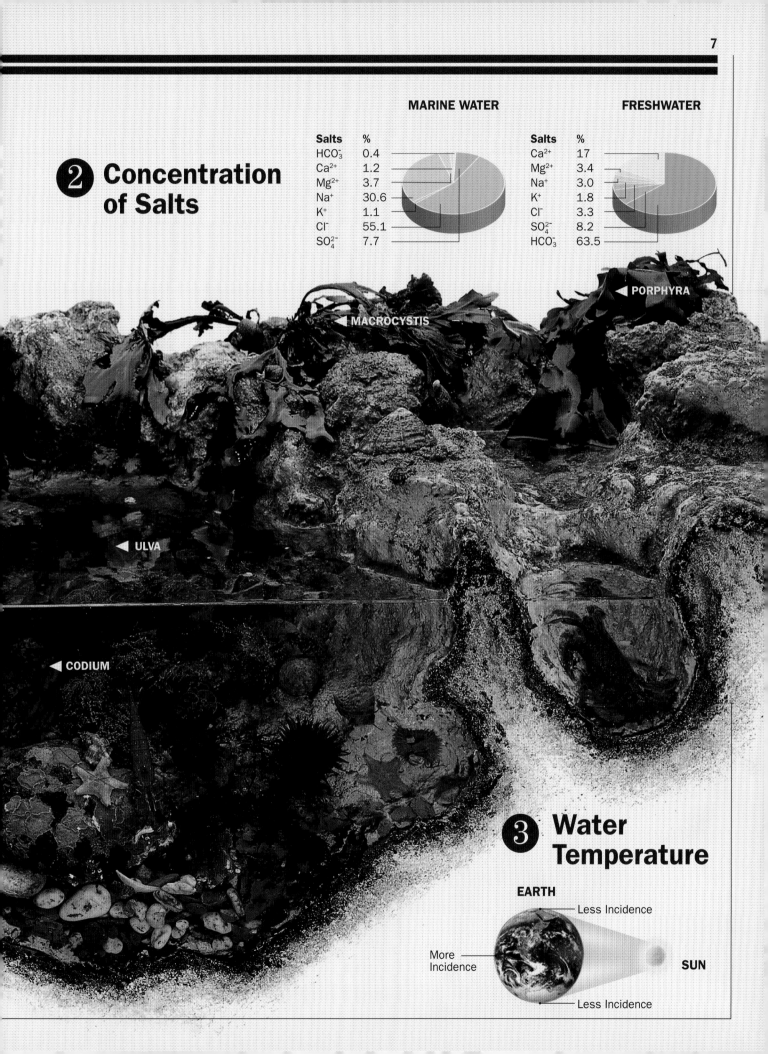

◀ PORPHYRA

MACROCYSTIS ▶

◀ ULVA

◀ CODIUM

❸ Water Temperature

EARTH

Less Incidence

More Incidence

SUN

Less Incidence

Aquatic Plants

These plants are especially adapted for living in ponds, streams, lakes, and rivers—places where other land plants cannot grow. Although aquatic plants belong to many different *families*, they have similar *adaptations*. They may be submerged or floating, with leaves above or below the water's surface.

Rooted Plants with Floating Leaves

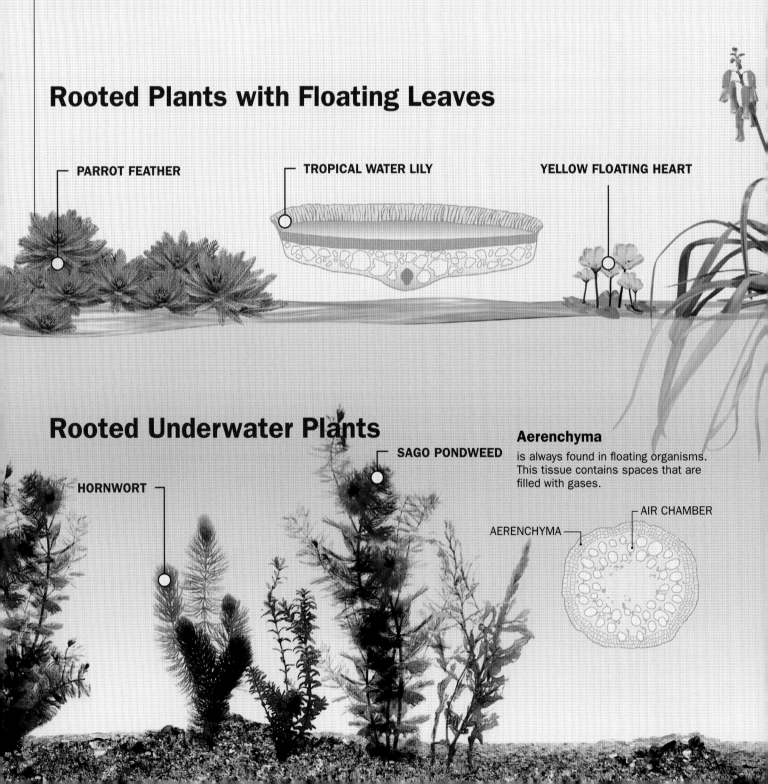

PARROT FEATHER

TROPICAL WATER LILY

YELLOW FLOATING HEART

Rooted Underwater Plants

SAGO PONDWEED

HORNWORT

Aerenchyma
is always found in floating organisms. This tissue contains spaces that are filled with gases.

AIR CHAMBER

AERENCHYMA

300 THE NUMBER OF WELL-KNOWN SPECIES OF WATER PLANTS

CATTAILS

Amphibious or Wetland Plants

LACHENALIA

ARROWHEAD

KNOTWEED

Submerged or Free

BLADDERWORT

EELGRASS

Life Began in the Sea

Invertebrates are not defined by any single common characteristic, but simply by not being vertebrates. Some 3.8 billion years ago, life arose in our planet's oceans. The species that inhabit the ocean waters show greater diversity than those found in other environments. Some forms of animal life, such as corals and sponges, are so simple that they are not able to move about on their own. Others, such as some *cephalopods*, show great intelligence and skill.

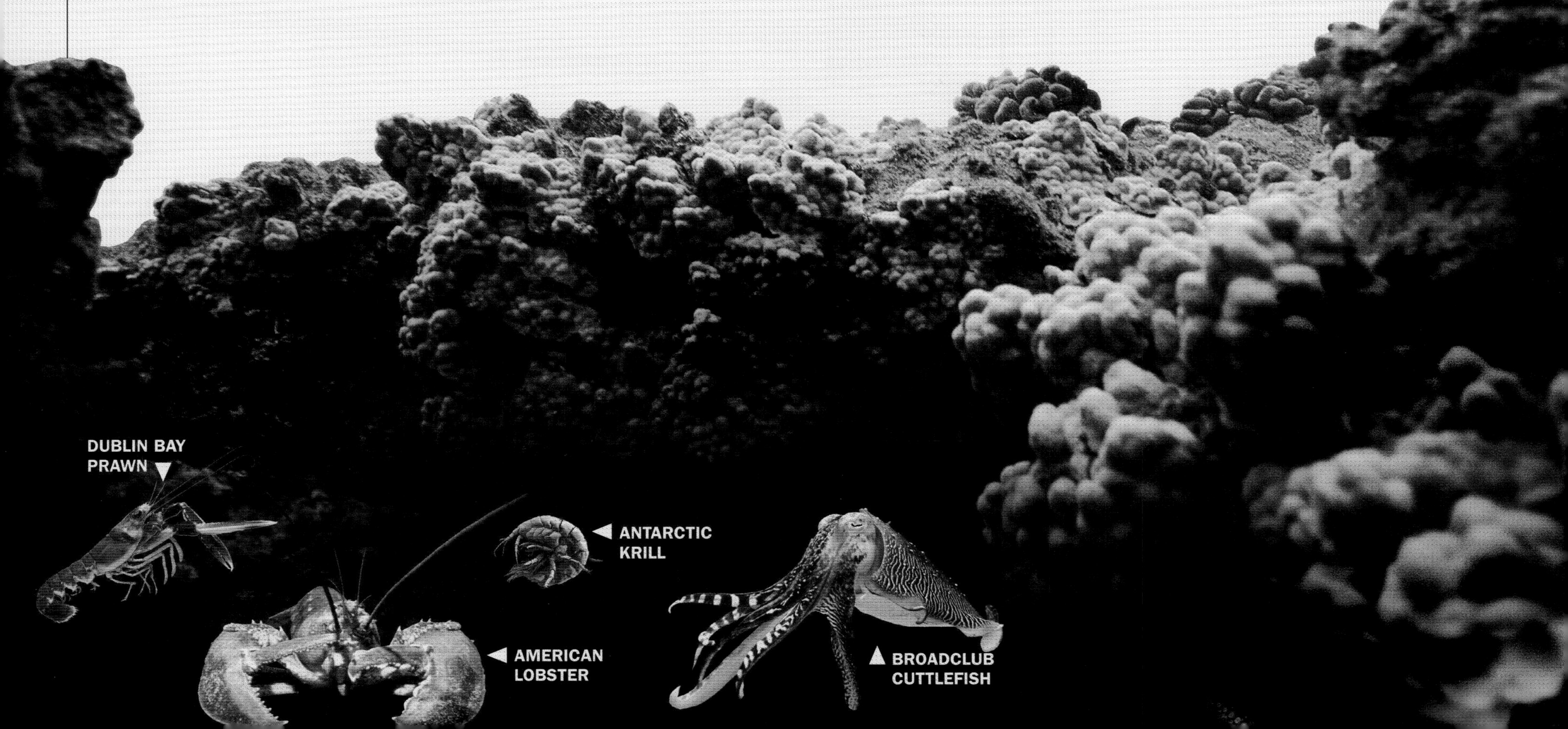

DUBLIN BAY PRAWN ▶

AMERICAN LOBSTER ◀

ANTARCTIC KRILL ◀

BROADCLUB CUTTLEFISH ◀

66 feet
(20 m) length
of the giant squid

▲ BIGFIN REEF SQUID
Male and female

▲ COMMON OCTOPUS

WHITE
JELLYFISH ▼   ▶ JELLYFISH

Unique Adaptation

In order to breathe underwater, invertebrates developed gills.

◀ SPONGE

▲ SEA CUCUMBER

RADIANT SEA URCHIN
AND URCHIN CRAB

◀ COMMON STARFISH

▼ TIGER COWRY

OYSTERS ◀

BEADLET
ANEMONE ▲

SEA SLUG ▼

RED
STARFISH ◀

▼ CHRISTMAS
TREE WORM

Radial Symmetry

Many of the numerous *invertebrates* on Earth live in the ocean. Some, such as *polyps* and jellyfish, have radial symmetry—that is, their bodies are structured around an axis. A typical *echinoderm* such as the starfish has tiny, flexible, tube-shaped legs arranged like the spokes of a wheel. The animal uses them to hold onto surfaces and to move. Sponges, on the other hand, are very simple, multiple-celled animals, with many small pores that they use to feed.

RADIAL SYMMETRY

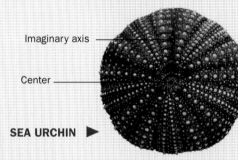

Imaginary axis

Center

SEA URCHIN ▶

Echinoderms

There are approximately

7,000

LIVING SPECIES AND 13,000 EXTINCT SPECIES OF ECHINODERMS.

ECHINODERM CLASSES

SEA URCHINS

STARFISH

BRITTLE STARS

SEA LILIES

SEA CUCUMBERS

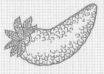

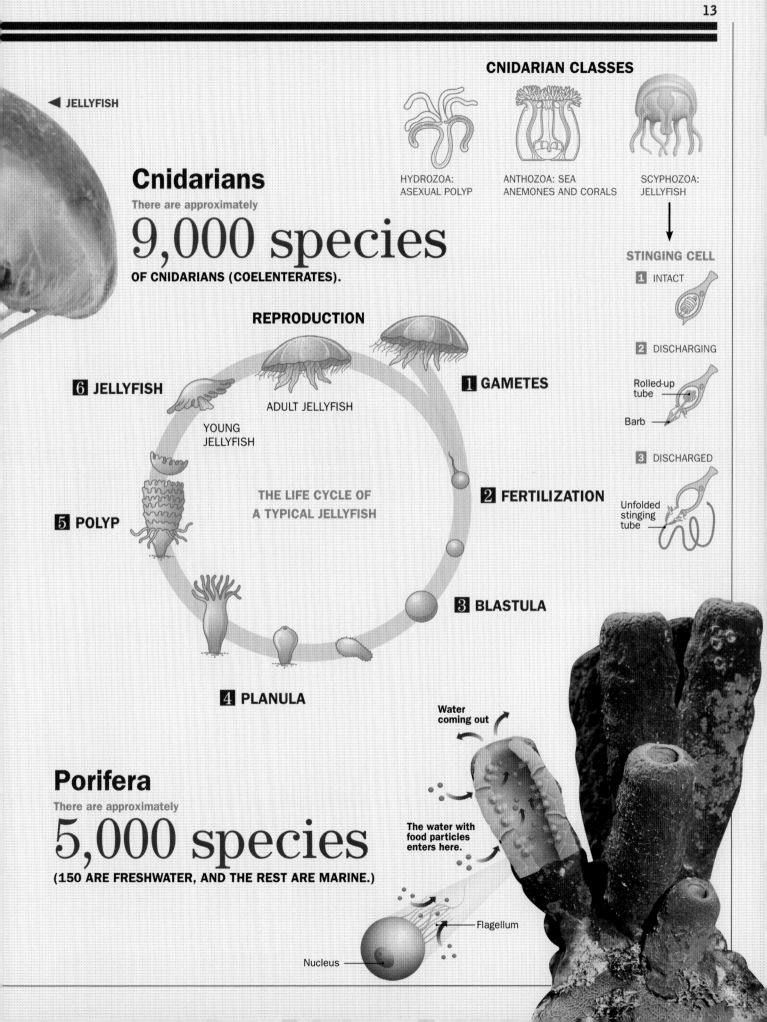

◀ JELLYFISH

Cnidarians

There are approximately

9,000 species

OF CNIDARIANS (COELENTERATES).

CNIDARIAN CLASSES

HYDROZOA: ASEXUAL POLYP

ANTHOZOA: SEA ANEMONES AND CORALS

SCYPHOZOA: JELLYFISH

STINGING CELL

1 INTACT

2 DISCHARGING

Rolled-up tube

Barb

3 DISCHARGED

Unfolded stinging tube

REPRODUCTION

6 JELLYFISH

ADULT JELLYFISH

YOUNG JELLYFISH

1 GAMETES

THE LIFE CYCLE OF
A TYPICAL JELLYFISH

5 POLYP

2 FERTILIZATION

3 BLASTULA

4 PLANULA

Porifera

There are approximately

5,000 species

(150 ARE FRESHWATER, AND THE REST ARE MARINE.)

Water coming out

The water with food particles enters here.

Flagellum

Nucleus

Marine Sediments

Sedimentary rocks can also form through the accumulation and lithification of organic remains. The most common example is coral *reefs*, which develop underwater, surrounding the coasts of many temperate seas. Many limestone rocks also originate this way; they are made of calcium carbonate (calcite) or calcium and magnesium (dolomite). Because of their porous consistency, they often serve as repositories for *fossil* fuels, which are also of organic origin. Other rocks, like coquina, form through the accumulation of fragments of marine shells, lithified over time as materials filled and cemented their interstices.

COQUINA ▶

◀ CALCITE

From Sediment to Rock

CORALS IN ARIZONA

Old Reefs

Current State Boundary

Current Coastal Boundary

Paleozoic Coastal Area

68° F (20° C)

MINIMUM WATER TEMPERATURE NEEDED FOR THE FORMATION OF CORAL

Coral Reefs

Barrier reef parallel
to the coast

Reef lagoon

Continental
shelf

HOW CORAL GROWS

Branched *Polyp*

Living Polyp

▼ **BRANCH CORAL**

▼ **BRAIN CORAL**

FLAT CORAL

3 feet (1 m)
**THE HEIGHT THAT A REEF CAN GROW
TOWARD THE SURFACE IN ONE YEAR**

Sea Carnival

Corals and anemones, together with jellyfish, make up the *phylum* Cnidaria. Some characteristics they share are their bright colors, tentacles that secrete stinging substances, and a digestive system with a common opening for ingestion and excretion—the simplest digestive system in the animal kingdom. All of these organisms are quite simple. Corals generally form *colonies*, large groups of small *polyps* that stay practically immobile and feed on *microorganisms* brought to them by water currents. Sea anemones, on the other hand, are solitary and can trap prey despite their limited locomotion.

Coral Reefs

HARD CORALS

SOFT CORALS

100 feet (30 m)
THE MOST COMMON DEPTH AT WHICH CORALS GROW

Tentacles

Mouth

Hard skeleton

Live tissue

Gastric cavity

Calcium carbonate

Connecting tissue

ADAPTATION OF SHAPE

Water flow

CONTRACTION DISTENSION EXTENSION

Tentacles

Column

Base

CORAL *POLYP*

Beautiful but Deadly

▼ SEA ANEMONE

TENTACLES

CLOWNFISH

MOUTH

BASAL DISC

GASTROVASCULAR CAVITY

Echinoderms

Echinoderms are one of the best-known groups of marine *invertebrates*. Sea urchins and starfish, despite their apparent differences, are part of the same group and share characteristics such as five-radial symmetry and the lack of a brain or eyes.

570 million years

THE LENGTH OF TIME ECHINODERMS HAVE BEEN IN EXISTENCE

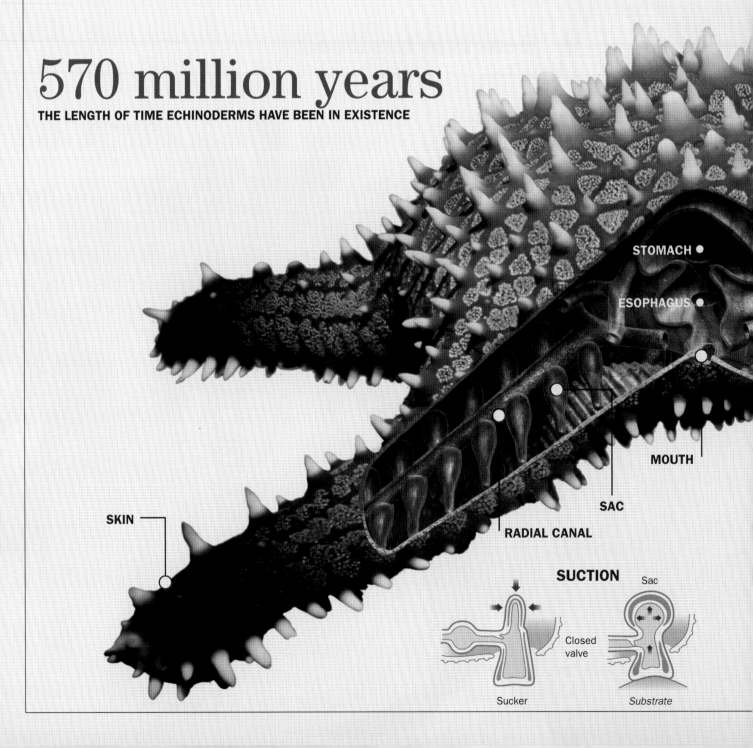

STOMACH ●

ESOPHAGUS ●

MOUTH

SAC

RADIAL CANAL

SKIN

SUCTION

Sac

Closed valve

Sucker

Substrate

Defense System

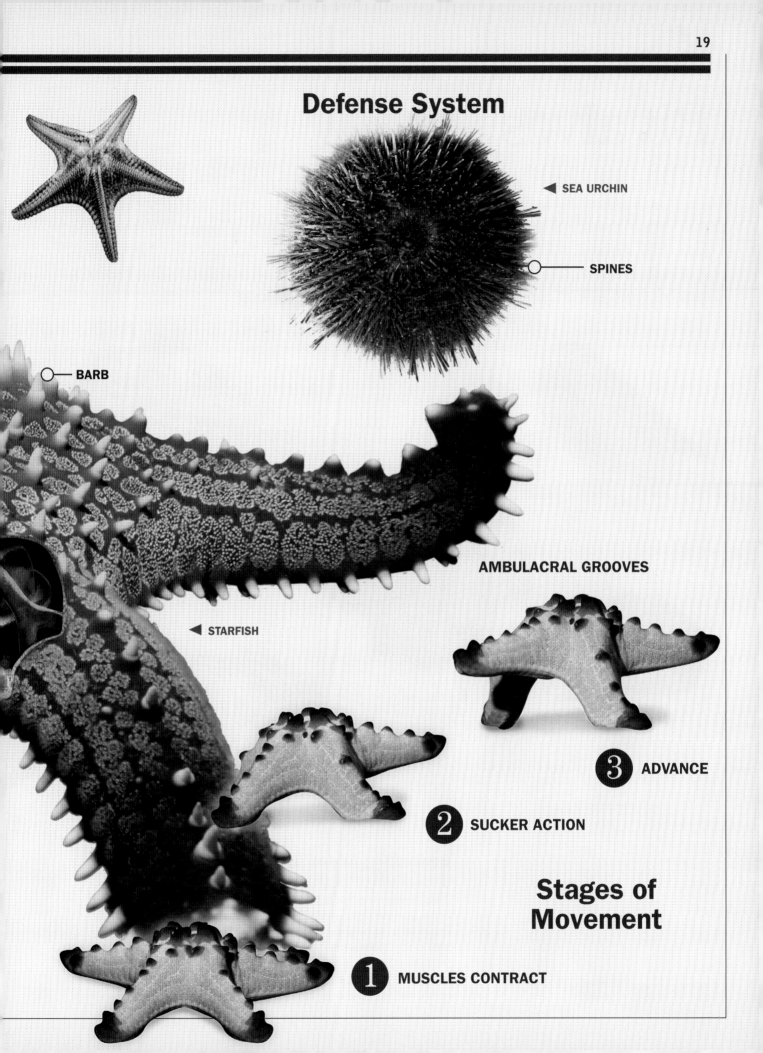

◄ SEA URCHIN

SPINES

BARB

AMBULACRAL GROOVES

◄ STARFISH

3 ADVANCE

2 SUCKER ACTION

Stages of Movement

1 MUSCLES CONTRACT

Bivalves

A bivalve is a *mollusk* with a shell divided into two halves. The two parts of the shell are joined by an elastic ligament that opens the shell, adductor muscles that close the shell, and the umbo, a system of ridges that helps the shell shut together. Almost all bivalves feed on *microorganisms*. Some bury themselves in the wet sand, digging small tunnels that let in water and food. The tunnels can be from a fraction of an inch long to over a yard long.

▲ MUSSEL

▲ OYSTER

▲ GREEN MUSSEL

▲ SCALLOP

▲ CLAM

UNDER THE SAND

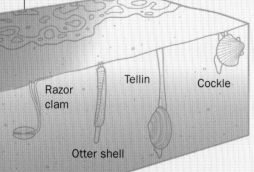

Razor clam

Tellin

Cockle

Otter shell

Generating Added Value

Bivalves are sought after and cultivated for their pearls. Pearls are said to be the queen of gems, because they were discovered over 4,000 years ago and were used as important symbols in many ancient cultures. In spite of their high price, pearls start out as a nuisance for the animal that creates them, which could be an oyster, a clam, or a mussel. Oysters produce the most valuable pearls, which are noted for their luster.

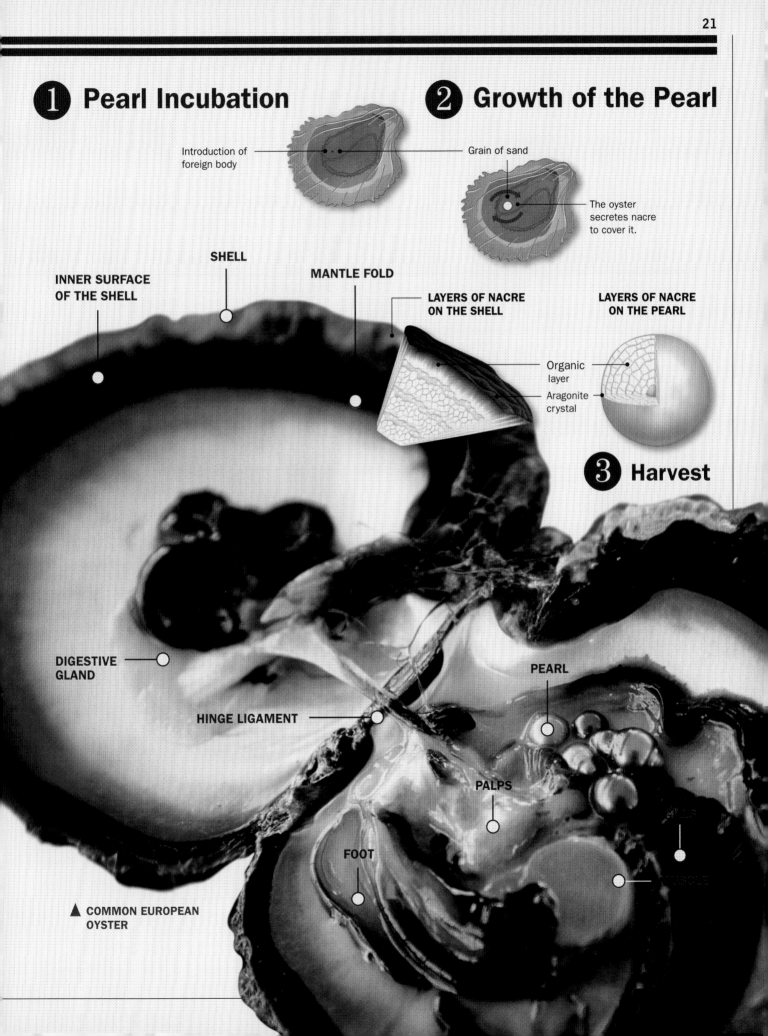

① Pearl Incubation

② Growth of the Pearl

Introduction of foreign body

Grain of sand

The oyster secretes nacre to cover it.

INNER SURFACE OF THE SHELL

SHELL

MANTLE FOLD

LAYERS OF NACRE ON THE SHELL

LAYERS OF NACRE ON THE PEARL

Organic layer

Aragonite crystal

③ Harvest

DIGESTIVE GLAND

HINGE LIGAMENT

PEARL

PALPS

FOOT

▲ COMMON EUROPEAN OYSTER

Powerful Tentacles

The eight-tentacled octopus is one of the few large ocean *cephalopods* to live in deep water. It is usually found on the rocky or sandy bottoms of shallow waters near the mouths of rivers. It generally moves slowly, sometimes moving in brief spurts, but it can reach great speeds when hunting or fleeing. Some are quite intelligent, having highly evolved brains.

▼ A Master of Color

EYES

HEAD

SKIN

1 The funnel muscles can act as a mechanism for fleeing. Rather than directing the funnel forward, though, the octopus directs it to advance toward its prey.

2 The tentacles stretch forward and outward as the octopus advances.

3 Using the wide area at the base of its tentacles, it envelops the prey.

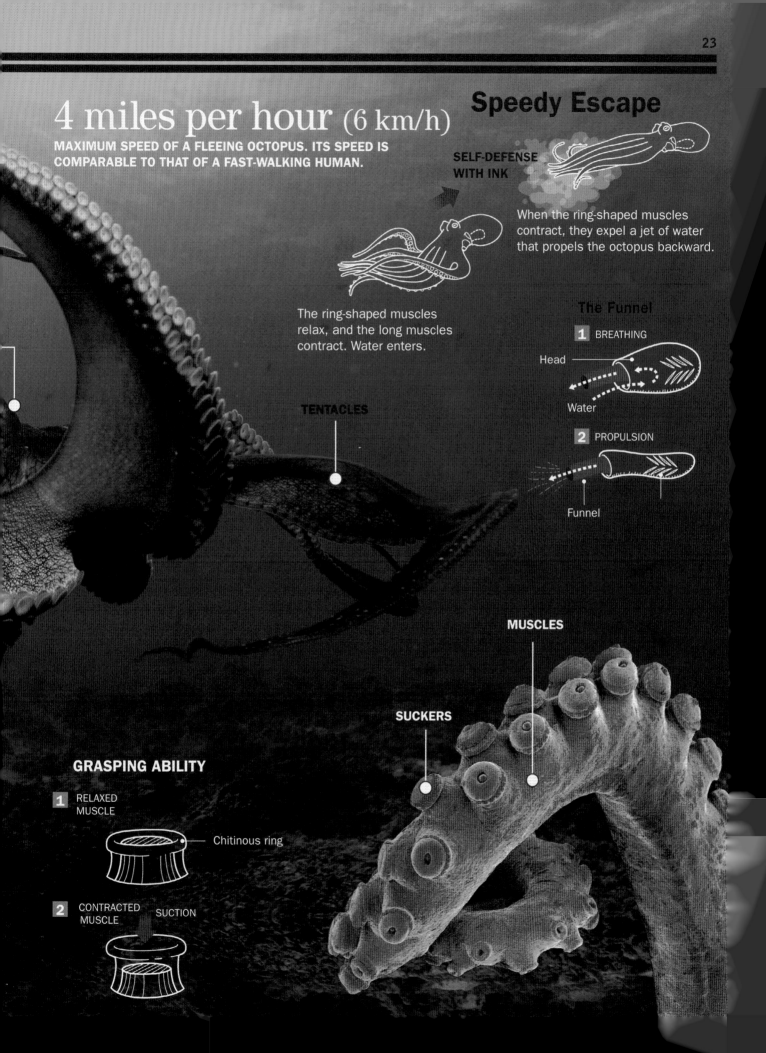

4 miles per hour (6 km/h)

MAXIMUM SPEED OF A FLEEING OCTOPUS. ITS SPEED IS COMPARABLE TO THAT OF A FAST-WALKING HUMAN.

Speedy Escape

SELF-DEFENSE WITH INK

When the ring-shaped muscles contract, they expel a jet of water that propels the octopus backward.

The ring-shaped muscles relax, and the long muscles contract. Water enters.

TENTACLES

The Funnel

1 BREATHING

Head

Water

2 PROPULSION

Funnel

MUSCLES

SUCKERS

GRASPING ABILITY

1 RELAXED MUSCLE

Chitinous ring

2 CONTRACTED MUSCLE — SUCTION

Colorful Armor

Even though they inhabit all known environments, *crustaceans* are most closely identified with the aquatic environment. Some crustaceans are very small: sea lice, for instance, are no larger than one hundredth of an inch (a quarter of a millimeter). The Japanese spider crab, on the other hand, is more than 9 feet (3 m) long with outstretched legs.

PINCERS

Wood Louse

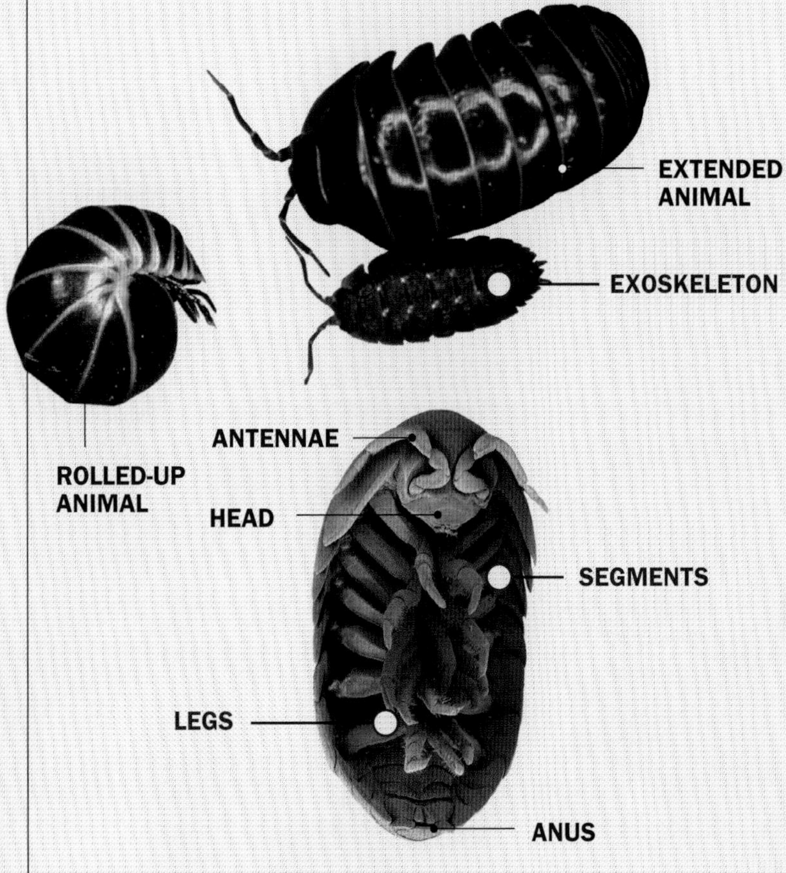

EXTENDED ANIMAL

EXOSKELETON

APPENDAGES

ROLLED-UP ANIMAL

ANTENNAE

HEAD

SEGMENTS

LEGS

ANUS

Barnacles

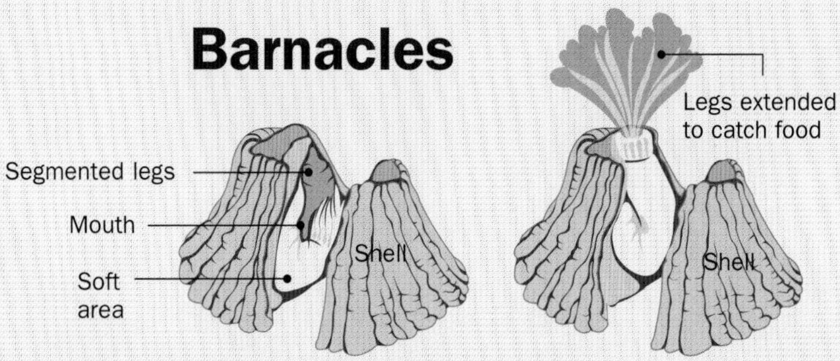

Segmented legs

Mouth

Soft area

Shell

Legs extended to catch food

Shell

◀ BARNACLE COLONY

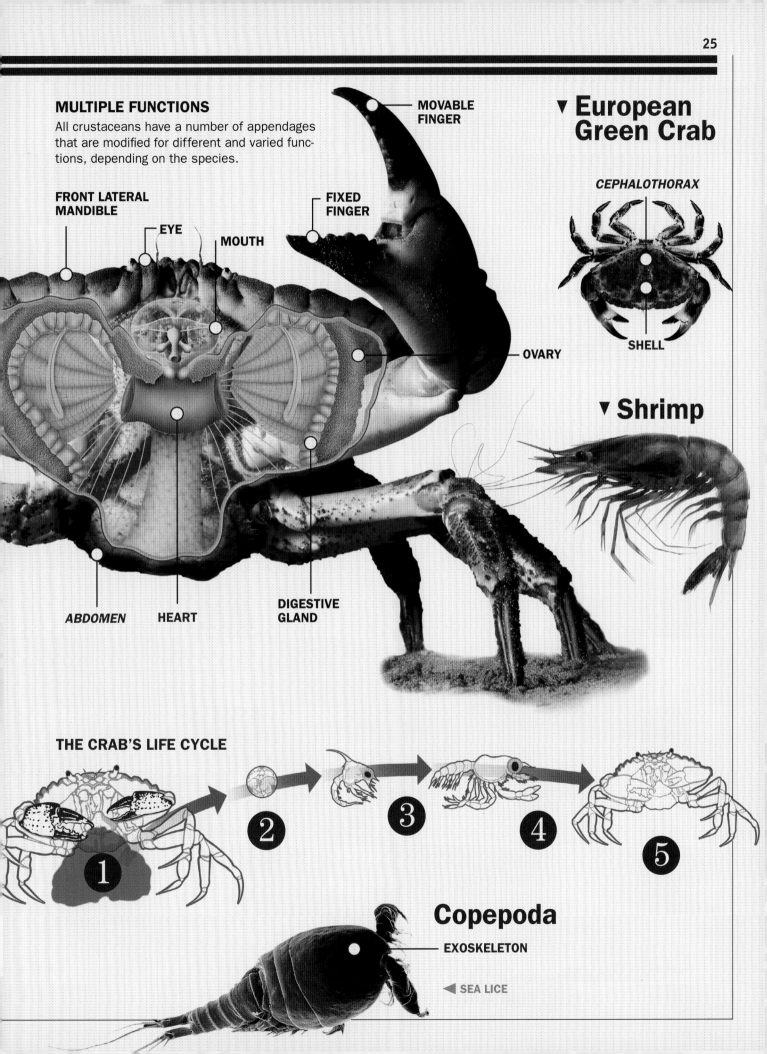

MULTIPLE FUNCTIONS

All crustaceans have a number of appendages that are modified for different and varied functions, depending on the species.

MOVABLE FINGER

▼ **European Green Crab**

FRONT LATERAL MANDIBLE

EYE

MOUTH

FIXED FINGER

CEPHALOTHORAX

SHELL

OVARY

ABDOMEN

HEART

DIGESTIVE GLAND

▼ **Shrimp**

THE CRAB'S LIFE CYCLE

1

2

3

4

5

Copepoda

EXOSKELETON

◄ SEA LICE

Sharp Front Legs

Crustaceans have appendages that generally branch in two directions and are adapted to aquatic life. Crustaceans have an articulated shell, which leaves two pairs of antennae uncovered. Crustaceans include lobsters, crabs, shrimp, and prawns, among other animals.

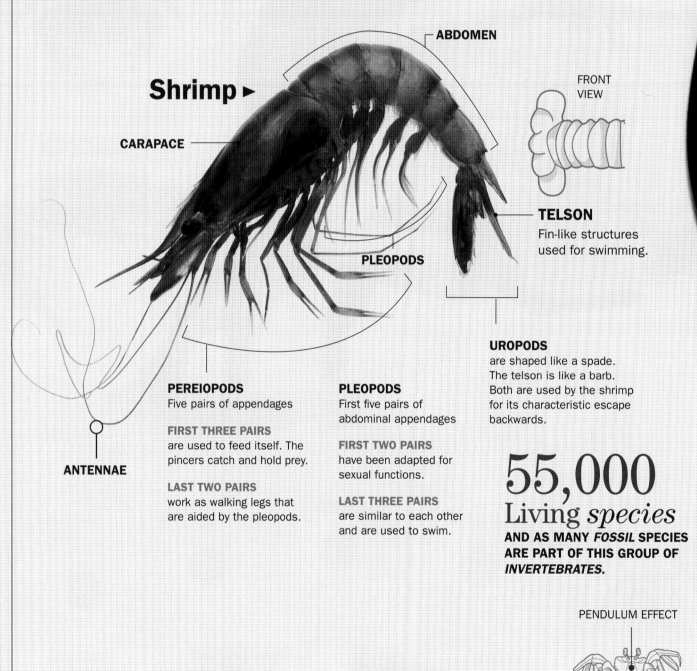

Shrimp ▶

ABDOMEN

FRONT VIEW

CARAPACE

TELSON
Fin-like structures used for swimming.

PLEOPODS

UROPODS
are shaped like a spade. The telson is like a barb. Both are used by the shrimp for its characteristic escape backwards.

ANTENNAE

PEREIOPODS
Five pairs of appendages

FIRST THREE PAIRS
are used to feed itself. The pincers catch and hold prey.

LAST TWO PAIRS
work as walking legs that are aided by the pleopods.

PLEOPODS
First five pairs of abdominal appendages

FIRST TWO PAIRS
have been adapted for sexual functions.

LAST THREE PAIRS
are similar to each other and are used to swim.

55,000
Living *species*
AND AS MANY *FOSSIL* SPECIES ARE PART OF THIS GROUP OF *INVERTEBRATES*.

PENDULUM EFFECT

Crab ▶

AT REST

SLOW WALK

◄ **Lobster**

3

**SMALL
CLAWS**

NERVES

ARTERY NETWORK

2

CUTTING CLAW
Cutting Edge

FLEXOR MUSCLE

TENDON

**WALKING
LEGS**

JOINTS AND LEVERS

1

CRUSHING CLAW
Teeth

Resistance
power

REBOUND EFFECT

FAST WALK

Joint

Muscle

Muscle

In the Middle of the Chain

Zooplankton include thousands of distinct species belonging to very different groups. These small, weakly swimming organisms are an extensive and varied community in the food network. The phytoplankton, which are capable of photosynthesis, provide food for the zooplankton. Phytoplankton also serve as food for echinoderms, crustaceans, and larval-stage fish. Once they grow up, the larvae serve as food for schools of small fish, which are in turn food for larger fish, including plankton-feeding whales.

Malacostraca

KRILL &

REAL SIZE
1.5 inches
(3.8 cm)

HOW IT FLEES

0 second

0.5 second

1 second

10 inches
(25 cm)

20 inches
(50 cm)

TROPHIC CHAIN

Tertiary
consumers — 10 — RIGHT WHALE

Secondary
consumers — 100 — OCTOPUSES, PENGUINS, FISH

Primary
consumers — 1,000 — ZOOPLANKTON

Producers — 10,000 — PHYTOPLANKTON

12,000
SPECIES OF COPEPODS

Copepods

REAL SIZE
0.08 inch (2 mm)

CYCLOPOID COPEPOD ▶

Branchiopods

◄ WATER FLEA
REAL SIZE
0.1 inch (3 mm)

Teeming Freshwater Environments

In rivers, ponds, lakes, lagoons, and swamps, many *invertebrate species* are adapted to life in the water but come from other habitats. Thus, water beetles breathe, not with *gills*, but with *spiracles*, the way land insects do. This means they must obtain a reserve of air or come to the surface to breathe. *Crustaceans* have mechanisms that protect them from losing salt in fresh water. With these adaptations, invertebrates make seemingly calm waters the scene of an intense struggle to survive.

▼ MOLTING DRAGONFLY

▼ EMPEROR DRAGONFLY

On the Border

▼ COMMON POND SKATER

▲ WATER BOATMAN (BACK SWIMMER)

One Species, Two Environments

LIFE CYCLE OF THE COMMON MOSQUITO

8% of insects live in water

ADULT **4**

PUPAE **3**

1 EGGS

THE PROCESS LASTS ABOUT ONE MONTH

2 LARVAE

▼ WATER MEASURER

▲ MAYFLY

GREAT POND SNAIL ▲

GREAT DIVING BEETLE ▲

▲ CADDISFLY LARVA

▲ MEDICINAL

COPEPOD

DIVING BELL SPIDER ▲

▲ TRICHODINA

BLOOD-FLUKES ▲

▲ ZOOPLANKTON

DRAGONFLY NYMPH ▲

▲ WHITE-CLAWED CRAYFISH

WATER BEETLE LARVA ▲

Most parasitic worms
are microscopic in size.
The ones shown here are
highly magnified.

Earliest Forms

About 470 million years ago, the first fish appeared. Unlike today's fish, they did not have a jawbone, fins, or scales. Hard plates covered the front part of the fish and formed a protective shield. They also had a solid, flexible dorsal spine that allowed them to propel themselves.

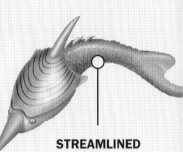

STREAMLINED SHAPE

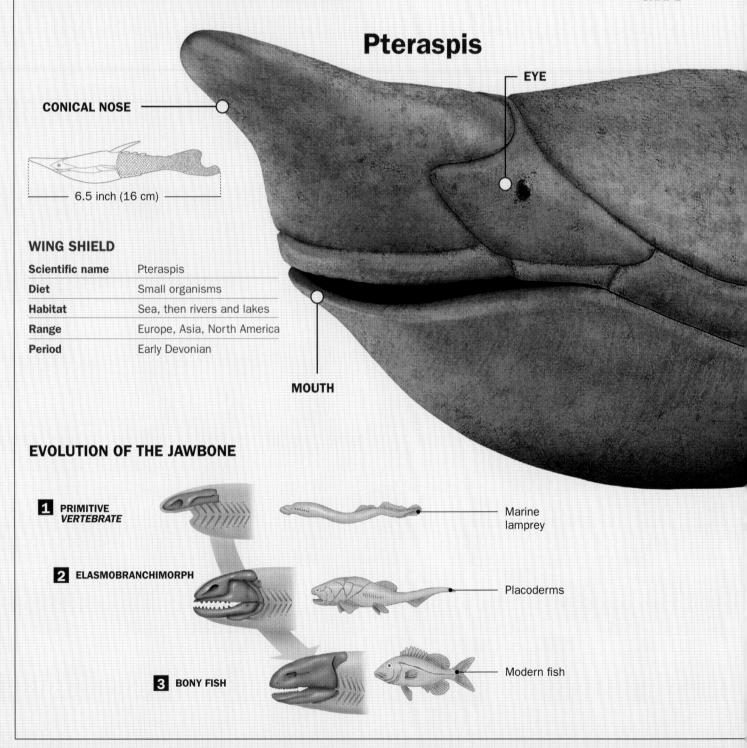

Pteraspis

CONICAL NOSE

EYE

6.5 inch (16 cm)

WING SHIELD

Scientific name	Pteraspis
Diet	Small organisms
Habitat	Sea, then rivers and lakes
Range	Europe, Asia, North America
Period	Early Devonian

MOUTH

EVOLUTION OF THE JAWBONE

1 PRIMITIVE VERTEBRATE

Marine lamprey

2 ELASMOBRANCHIMORPH

Placoderms

3 BONY FISH

Modern fish

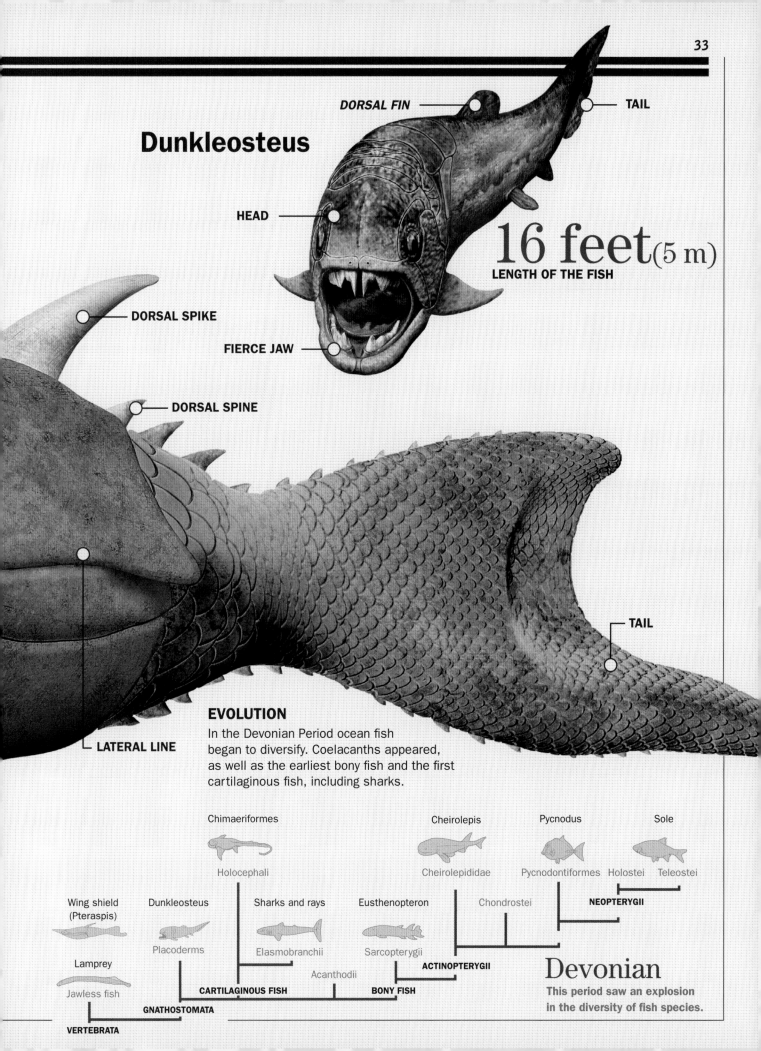

Dunkleosteus

DORSAL FIN

TAIL

HEAD

16 feet (5 m)
LENGTH OF THE FISH

DORSAL SPIKE

FIERCE JAW

DORSAL SPINE

TAIL

LATERAL LINE

EVOLUTION

In the Devonian Period ocean fish began to diversify. Coelacanths appeared, as well as the earliest bony fish and the first cartilaginous fish, including sharks.

Chimaeriformes

Holocephali

Cheirolepis

Cheirolepididae

Pycnodus

Pycnodontiformes

Sole

Holostei   Teleostei

NEOPTERYGII

Wing shield (Pteraspis)

Dunkleosteus

Placoderms

Sharks and rays

Elasmobranchii

Eusthenopteron

Sarcopterygii

Chondrostei

ACTINOPTERYGII

Lamprey

Jawless fish

Acanthodii

CARTILAGINOUS FISH

BONY FISH

GNATHOSTOMATA

Devonian
This period saw an explosion in the diversity of fish species.

VERTEBRATA

Distinguishing Features

Similar characteristics define nearly all fish, with a few rare exceptions. These aquatic animals are designed to live underwater, and they have a jawbone and lidless eyes and are cold-blooded. They breathe through *gills* and are vertebrates—that is, they have a spinal column. They live in the oceans, from the poles to the equator, as well as in bodies of fresh water and in streams. Some fish migrate, but very few can pass from salt water to fresh water or vice versa. Their fins enable them to swim and move in different directions.

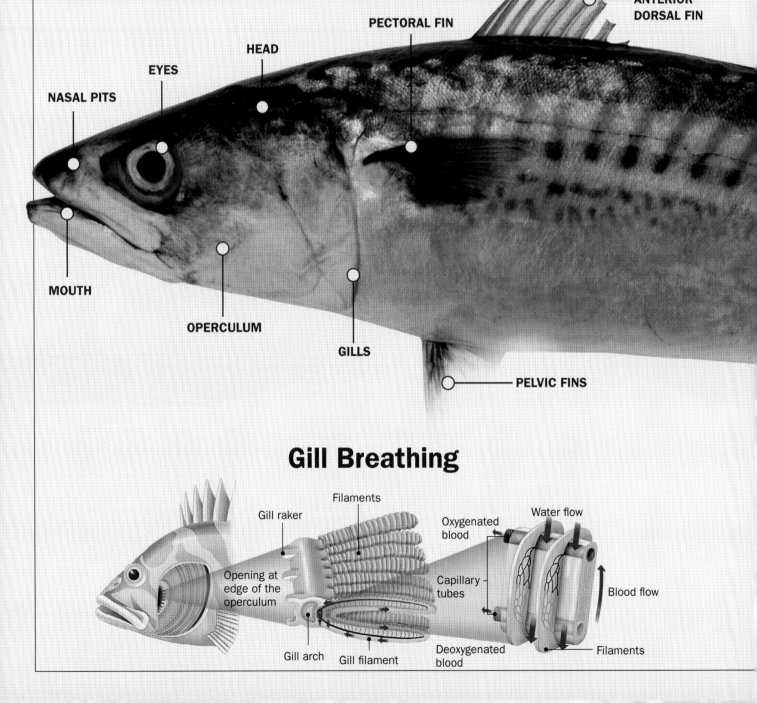

ANTERIOR DORSAL FIN

PECTORAL FIN

HEAD

EYES

NASAL PITS

MOUTH

OPERCULUM

GILLS

PELVIC FINS

Gill Breathing

Filaments

Gill raker

Oxygenated blood

Water flow

Opening at edge of the operculum

Capillary tubes

Blood flow

Gill arch   Gill filament

Deoxygenated blood

Filaments

SEA LAMPREY ▼

COELACANTH ▶

JUST CARTILAGE

25,000

Is the number of known fish species, making up nearly one half of all chordate species.

SCALES

POSTERIOR DORSAL FIN

▲ **RAY**

ANAL FIN

TAIL MUSCLE

LATERAL LINE

▼ **ATLANTIC MACKEREL**
This fish has no teeth. It lives in temperate waters, and its meat is considered delicious. It can live for more than 10 years.

CAUDAL FIN

In Action

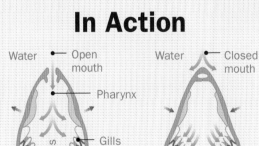

Water — Open mouth

Pharynx

Gills

Esophagus

Closed operculum

Water — Closed mouth

Open operculum

Cartilaginous

As indicated by the name, the skeleton of cartilaginous fish is made of cartilage, a flexible, durable substance that is softer than bone. They have jaws and teeth, which are usually hard and sharp. Their body is covered with hard ⬛⬛⬛⬛. However, they lack a characteristic shared by most ⬛⬛⬛⬛⬛—the ⬛⬛⬛⬛⬛⬛⬛, an organ that helps fish to float. Their ⬛⬛⬛⬛⬛⬛, tail, and flat head give this group a streamlined profile.

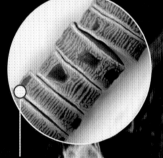

2,650 pounds
(1.2 metric tons)
NORMAL WEIGHT OF A SHARK

Nostril

Surface pore

Heat-generating muscles

Sensory cells

Nerves

Gelatinous tract

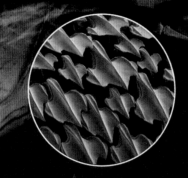

SCALES

IN SOME SHARK SPECIES, THE YOUNG
DEVELOP WITHIN THE FEMALE, INSIDE A
STRUCTURE SIMILAR TO A PLACENTA.

GILL SLITS

HETEROCERCAL TAIL

Chimaerae

CHIMAERAS

Elegant Contours

Rays are cartilaginous fish related to sharks. They have the same skeletal structure, the same number and type of fins, and similarly shaped *gill* slits. They are distinct in that their gill slits are on the underside of the body, which is flat with *pectoral fins* joined to the trunk in the shape of a disk. They have a variety of colors, with spots and blotches. They often burrow into the mud of warm seas.

Tail

Pectoral fin

▲ **RAY**

Head

POISONOUS TAIL

BLUE LINES

Flying Through the Water

ROUGH RAY

PECTORAL FINS

Tail — is slender and lacks the strength for swimming.

Blue-spotted Ribbontail Ray

12.4 miles per hour
(20 km/h)

Smiling Face

Nasal orifices

Hornlike mouth

Gill arch

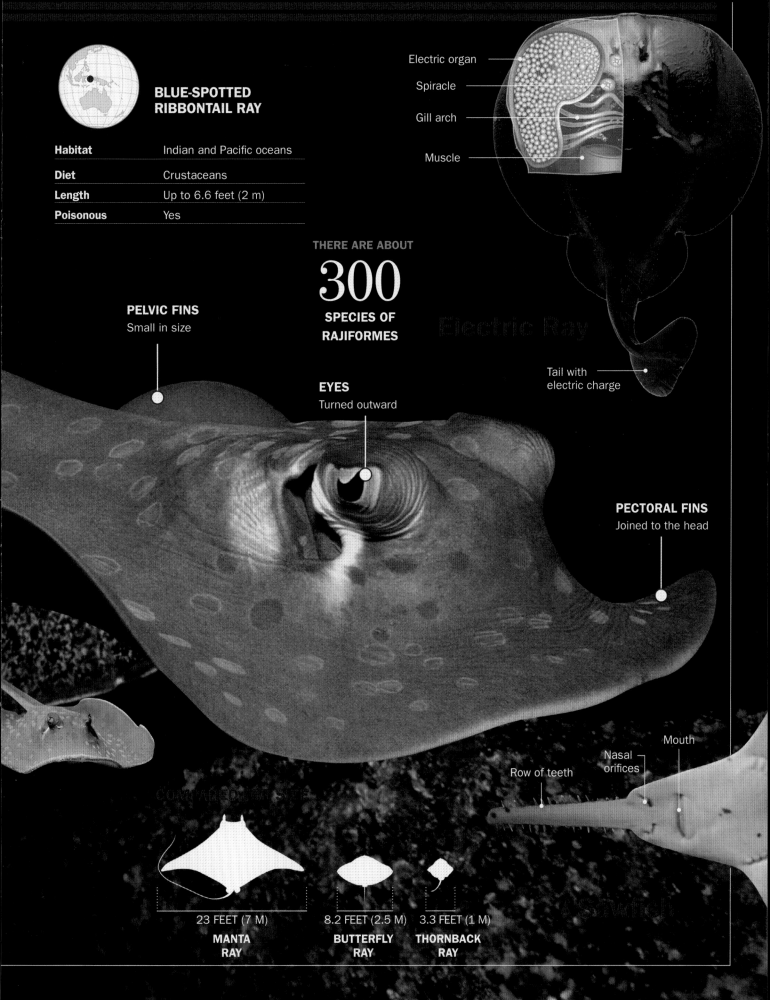

BLUE-SPOTTED RIBBONTAIL RAY

Habitat	Indian and Pacific oceans
Diet	Crustaceans
Length	Up to 6.6 feet (2 m)
Poisonous	Yes

Electric organ
Spiracle
Gill arch
Muscle

Electric Ray

THERE ARE ABOUT

300

SPECIES OF
RAJIFORMES

PELVIC FINS
Small in size

EYES
Turned outward

Tail with
electric charge

PECTORAL FINS
Joined to the head

Mouth
Nasal
orifices
Row of teeth

COMPARED BY SIZE

23 FEET (7 M)
**MANTA
RAY**

8.2 FEET (2.5 M)
**BUTTERFLY
RAY**

3.3 FEET (1 M)
**THORNBACK
RAY**

Deadly Weapon

One of the greatest predators in the ocean is the great white shark, easily identified by its distinctive white coloring, black eyes, and fierce teeth and jaws. Many biologists believe that attacks on humans result from the shark's exploratory behavior, because these fish often lift their heads above the water and explore things by biting them. This activity is often dangerous because of the sharpness of the sharks' teeth and the strength of their jaws. Great white sharks are implicated in most fatal shark attacks on humans, especially on surfers and divers.

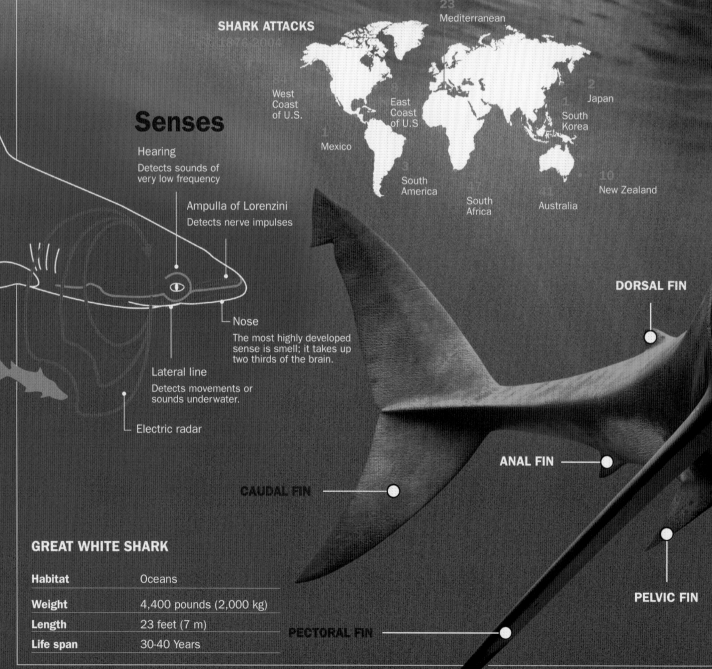

SHARK ATTACKS

23 Mediterranean

West Coast of U.S.

East Coast of U.S

2 Japan

1 South Korea

1 Mexico

3 South America

17 South Africa

41 Australia

10 New Zealand

Senses

Hearing
Detects sounds of very low frequency

Ampulla of Lorenzini
Detects nerve impulses

Nose
The most highly developed sense is smell; it takes up two thirds of the brain.

Lateral line
Detects movements or sounds underwater.

Electric radar

DORSAL FIN

ANAL FIN

CAUDAL FIN

PELVIC FIN

PECTORAL FIN

GREAT WHITE SHARK

Habitat	Oceans
Weight	4,400 pounds (2,000 kg)
Length	23 feet (7 m)
Life span	30-40 Years

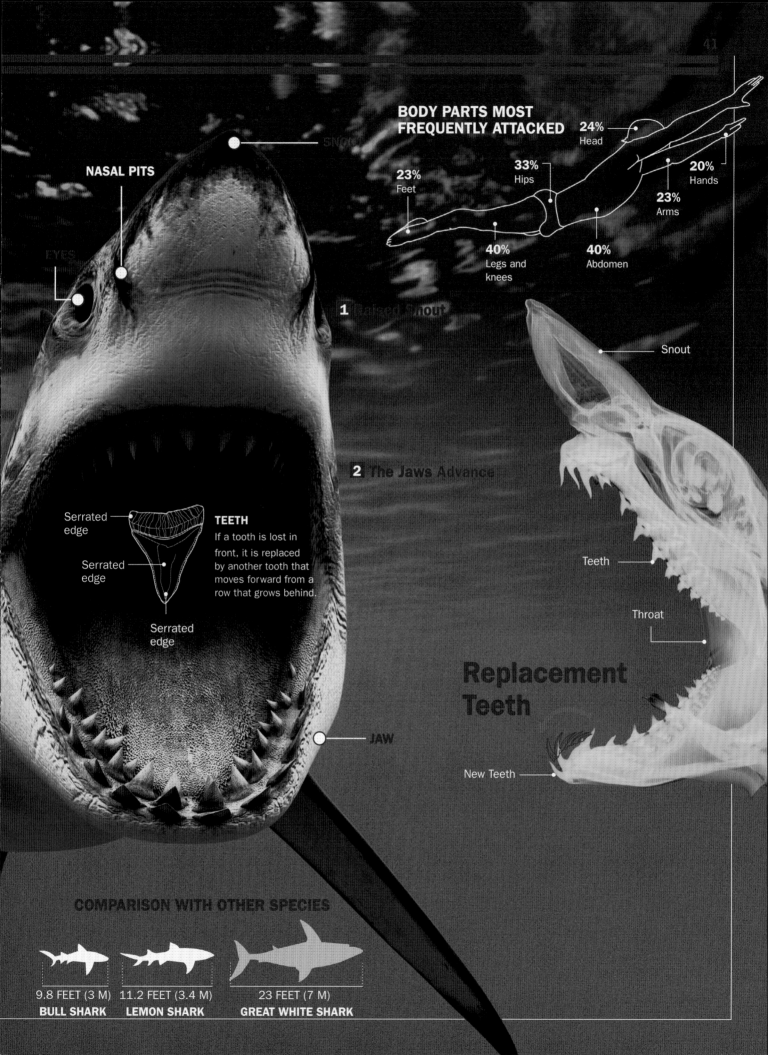

NASAL PITS

EYES

SNOUT

BODY PARTS MOST FREQUENTLY ATTACKED

24% Head

33% Hips

23% Feet

20% Hands

23% Arms

40% Legs and knees

40% Abdomen

1 Raised Snout

Snout

2 The Jaws Advance

Serrated edge

Serrated edge

Serrated edge

TEETH

If a tooth is lost in front, it is replaced by another tooth that moves forward from a row that grows behind.

Teeth

Throat

Replacement Teeth

JAW

New Teeth

COMPARISON WITH OTHER SPECIES

9.8 FEET (3 M)
BULL SHARK

11.2 FEET (3.4 M)
LEMON SHARK

23 FEET (7 M)
GREAT WHITE SHARK

Bony Fish

Bony fish have evolved and diversified more than any other group of fish in the past few million years. Their skeletons are small but firm. Flexible fins enable them to control their movements with precision. The various species of bony fish have adapted to a wide variety of environments and even to extreme conditions.

Solid Structure

LACRIMAL BONE

UPPER JAW

LOWER JAW

EYE SOCKET

OPERCULAR BONES

CLAVICLE

PELVIC FIN

DORSAL FIN

Actinopterygii

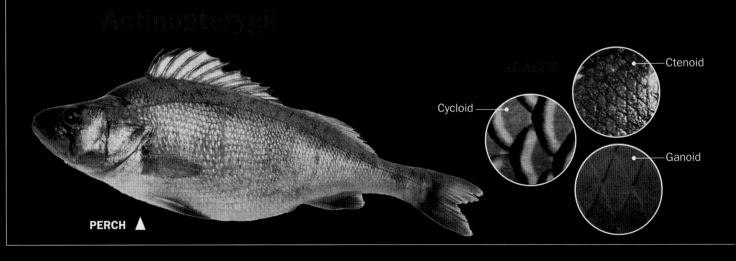

SCALES

Cycloid

Ctenoid

Ganoid

PERCH ▲

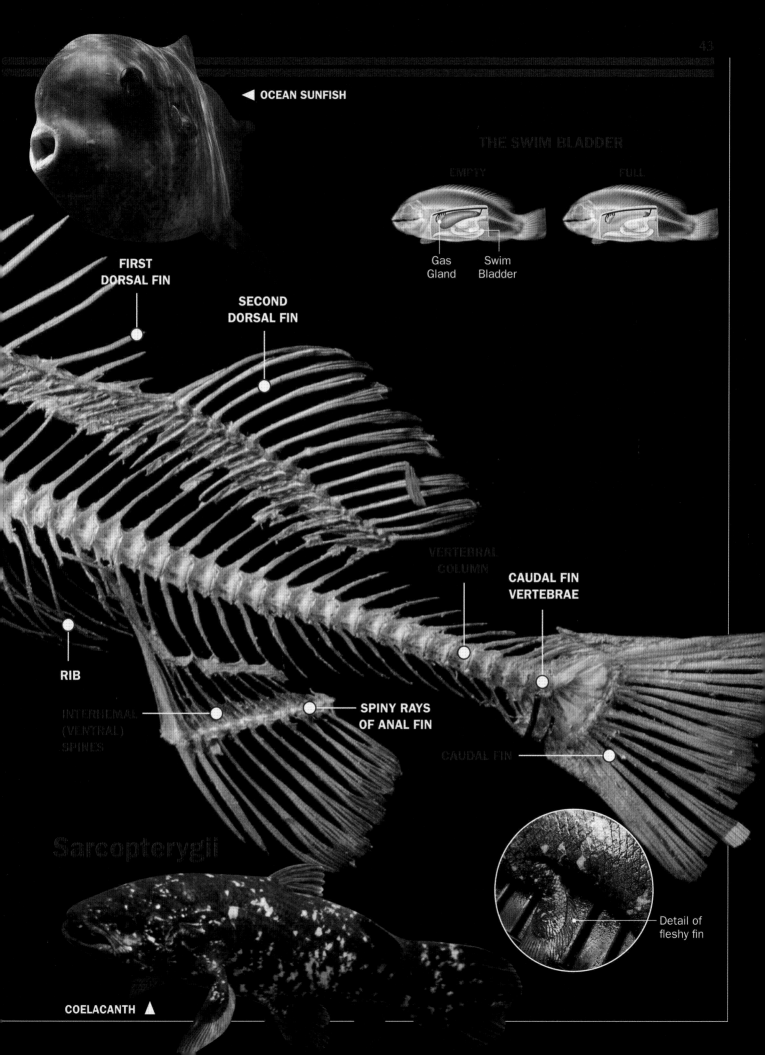

◄ OCEAN SUNFISH

THE SWIM BLADDER

EMPTY

FULL

Gas Gland

Swim Bladder

FIRST DORSAL FIN

SECOND DORSAL FIN

VERTEBRAL COLUMN

CAUDAL FIN VERTEBRAE

RIB

INTERHEMAL (VENTRAL) SPINES

SPINY RAYS OF ANAL FIN

CAUDAL FIN

Sarcopterygii

Detail of fleshy fin

COELACANTH ▲

Extremities

A fish can control its motion, direction, and stability by means of its fins and tail. Anatomically these are extensions of the skin beyond the body and, in most bony fish, are supported by rays. The fins reveal much about the life of each fish. Thin fins with a split tail indicate that the animal moves very quickly, or it may need them to cover great distances. On the other hand, fish that live among rocks and reefs near the ocean floor have broad lateral fins and large tails.

**SIAMESE ▲
FIGHTING FISH**

FIN RAYS ─○

Homocercal Tail

The spinal column ends
in a broadened structure.

**GREY REEF ▶
SHARK**

1/8 The proportion of the length of a salmon's
homocercal tail with respect to its body

The Typical Tail

The vast majority of bony fish
have homocercal tails.

Heterocercal Tail

The shark's spine extends into
the upper lobe of the caudal fin.

1/3 The proportion of the lower lobe of
the tail to the upper lobe of the tail

The lower lobe is smaller
and is merely a projection
to the side of the spine.

SALMON ▶

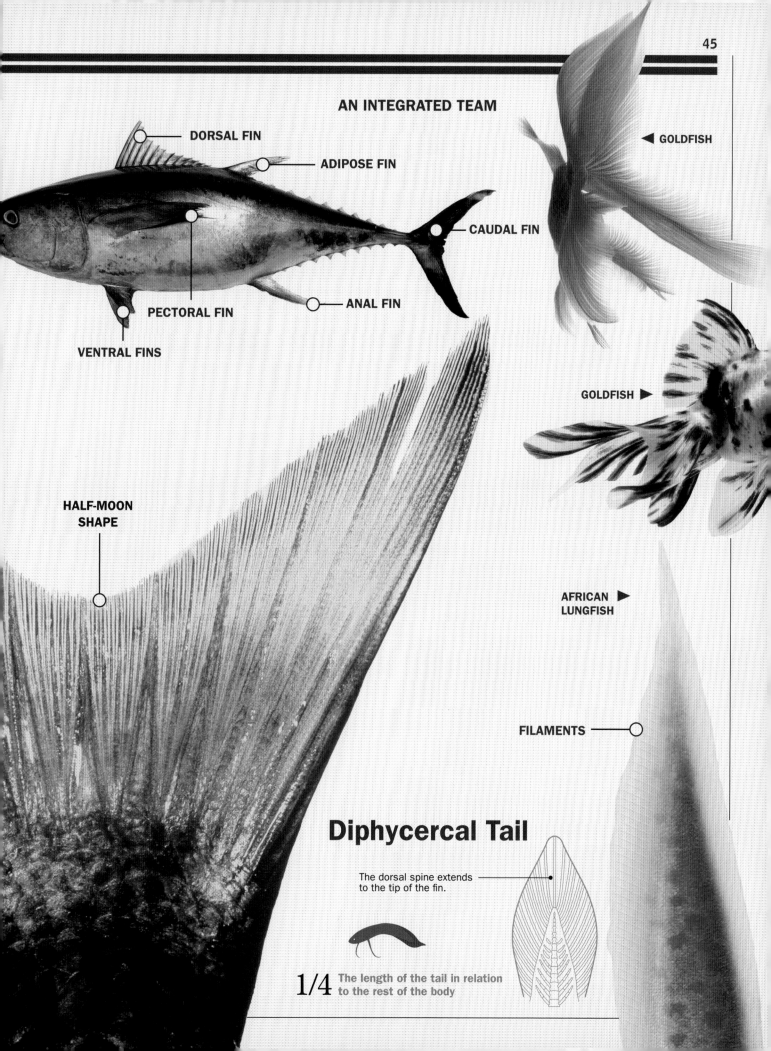

AN INTEGRATED TEAM

DORSAL FIN

ADIPOSE FIN

PECTORAL FIN

VENTRAL FINS

ANAL FIN

CAUDAL FIN

GOLDFISH

GOLDFISH ▶

AFRICAN LUNGFISH ▶

HALF-MOON SHAPE

FILAMENTS

Diphycercal Tail

The dorsal spine extends to the tip of the fin.

1/4 The length of the tail in relation to the rest of the body

The Art of Swimming

To swim, fish move in three dimensions: forward and back, left and right, and up and down. The main control surfaces that fish use for maneuvering are the fins, including the tail, or *caudal fin*. To change direction, the fish tilts the control surfaces at an angle to the water current. The fish must also keep its balance in the water; it accomplishes this by moving its paired and unpaired fins.

UPSIDE-DOWN CATFISH ▲

MUSCLES

GREAT WHITE SHARK ▲

Red muscles

Larger white muscles

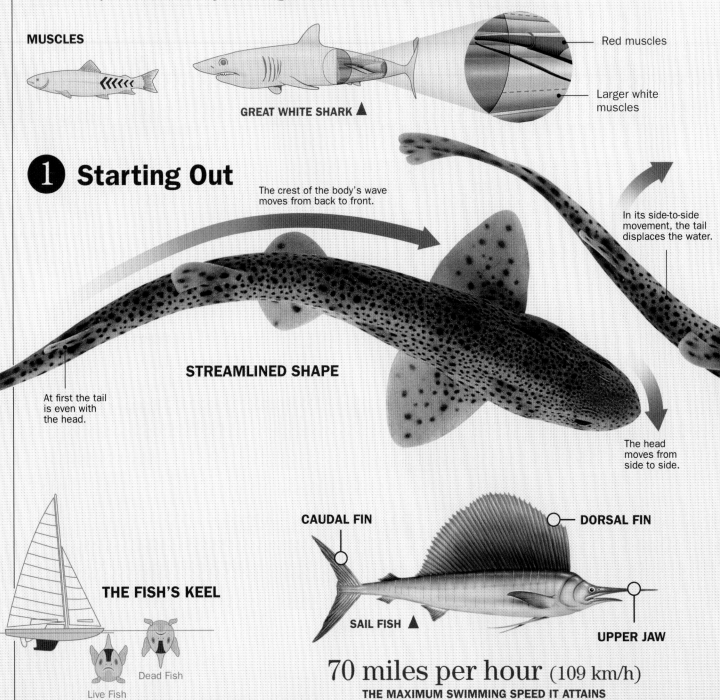

① Starting Out

The crest of the body's wave moves from back to front.

In its side-to-side movement, the tail displaces the water.

STREAMLINED SHAPE

At first the tail is even with the head.

The head moves from side to side.

THE FISH'S KEEL

Live Fish

Dead Fish

CAUDAL FIN

DORSAL FIN

SAIL FISH ▲

UPPER JAW

70 miles per hour (109 km/h)
THE MAXIMUM SWIMMING SPEED IT ATTAINS

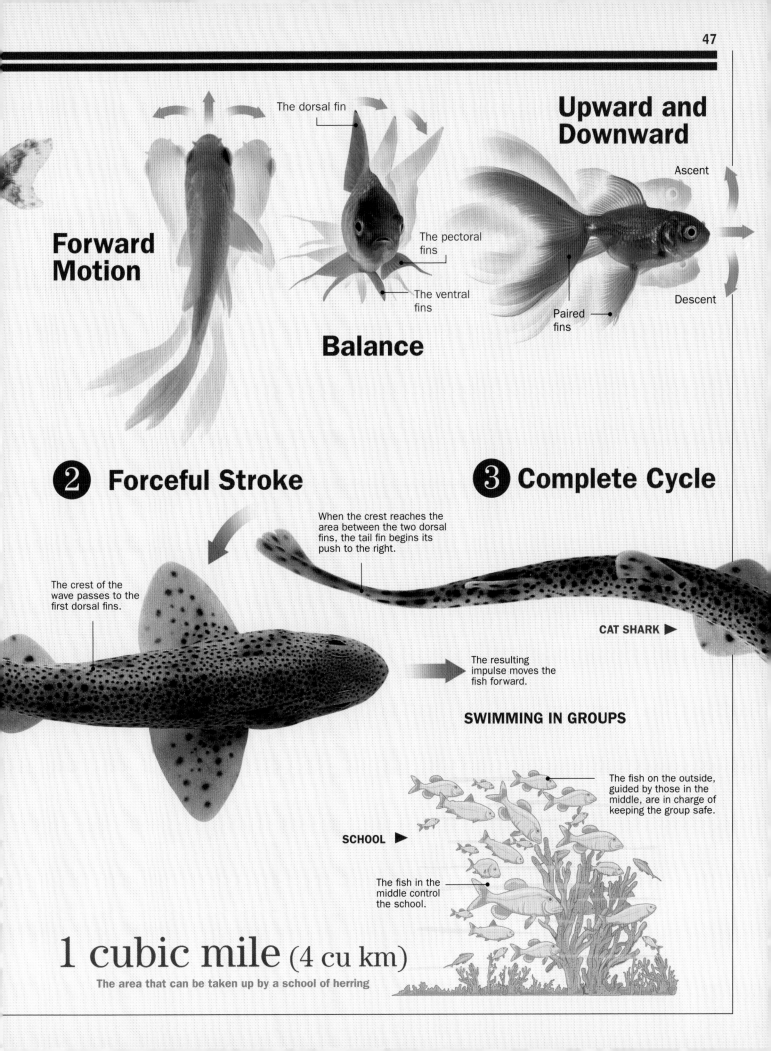

Forward Motion

The dorsal fin

Balance

The pectoral fins

The ventral fins

Upward and Downward

Ascent

Paired fins

Descent

② Forceful Stroke

When the crest reaches the area between the two dorsal fins, the tail fin begins its push to the right.

The crest of the wave passes to the first dorsal fins.

③ Complete Cycle

CAT SHARK ▶

The resulting impulse moves the fish forward.

SWIMMING IN GROUPS

The fish on the outside, guided by those in the middle, are in charge of keeping the group safe.

SCHOOL ▶

The fish in the middle control the school.

1 cubic mile (4 cu km)

The area that can be taken up by a school of herring

You Are What You Eat

Most fish feed in their natural environment, the larger fish eating the smaller ones, and the smallest sea creatures feeding on marine plants. A fish's mouth gives many clues about its feeding habits. Large, strong teeth indicate a diet of shellfish or coral; pointed teeth belong to a hunting fish; and a large mouth that is open while the fish swims is that of a filterer. Some _____ can also trap food that lives outside the water: trout, for example, hunt flies.

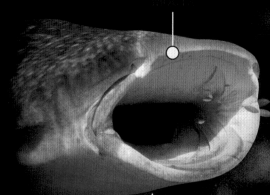

▲ WHALE SHARK

▲ PIRANHA

Plants

Life in the water is based on _____, which is eaten by zooplankton. These are in turn eaten by fish, all the way up to the large marine _____.

SUCKERS

▲ REMORA

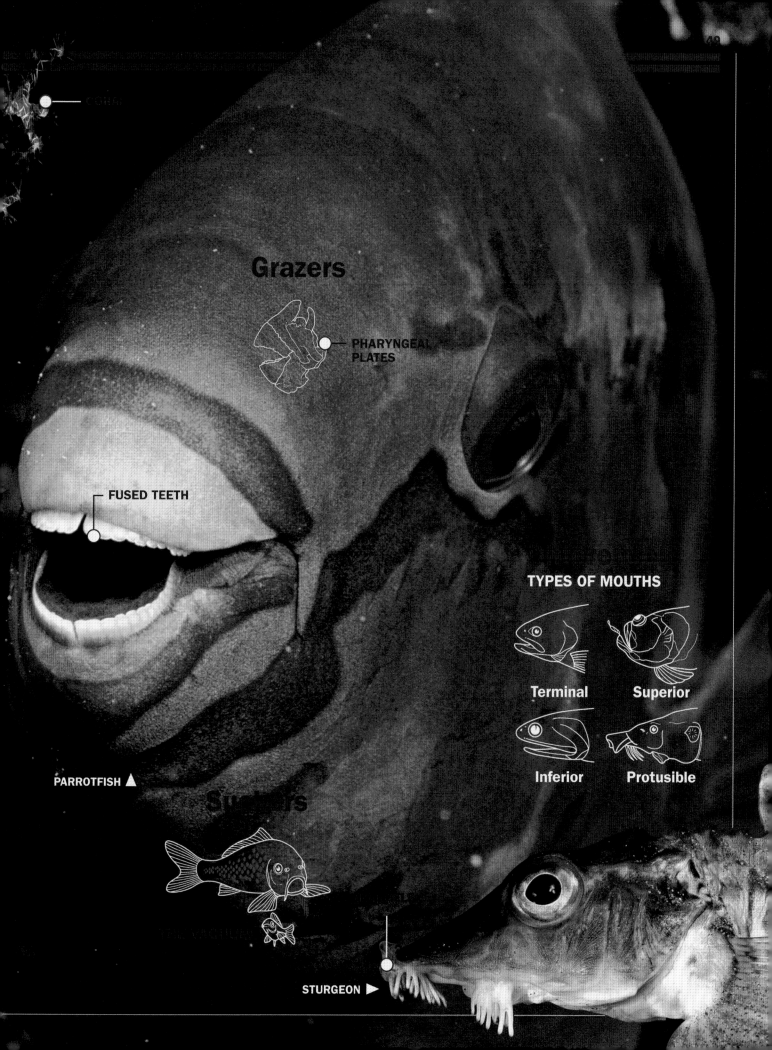

Grazers

PHARYNGEAL PLATES

FUSED TEETH

PARROTFISH ▲

Suckers

TYPES OF MOUTHS

Terminal   Superior

Inferior   Protusible

STURGEON ▶

Time to Eat

Most fish feed within their aquatic environment. Some *species*, however, seek their food outside the water. The best-known example is the archerfish, which shoots streams of water from its mouth to knock spiders and flies off nearby plants and into the water. The African butterfly fish eats flying insects, which it traps after a brief flight. The river hatchetfish has a similar strategy: its long *pectoral fins* and flattened body enable it to make great leaps.

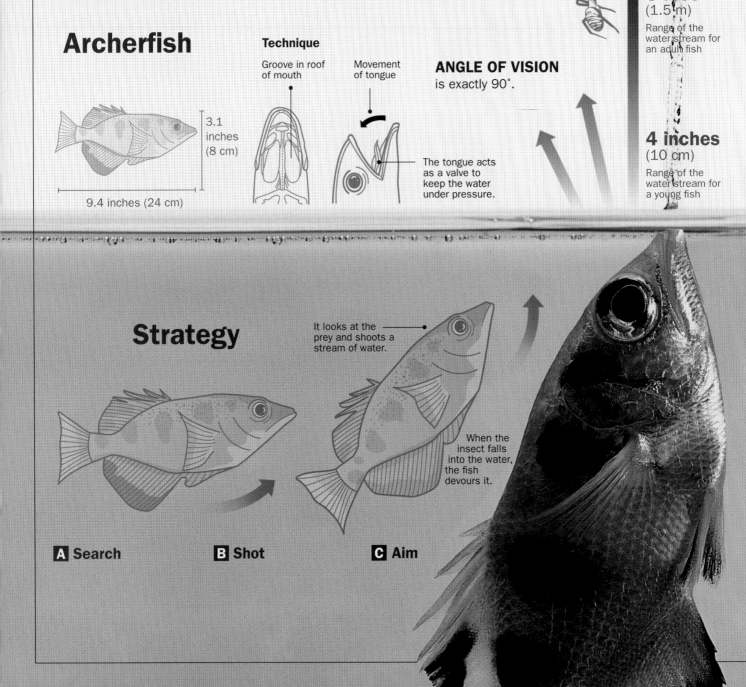

Archerfish

3.1 inches (8 cm)

9.4 inches (24 cm)

Technique

Groove in roof of mouth

Movement of tongue

The tongue acts as a valve to keep the water under pressure.

ANGLE OF VISION is exactly 90°.

5 feet (1.5 m)
Range of the water stream for an adult fish

4 inches (10 cm)
Range of the water stream for a young fish

Strategy

It looks at the prey and shoots a stream of water.

When the insect falls into the water, the fish devours it.

Ⓐ Search   **Ⓑ Shot**   **Ⓒ Aim**

Its prey includes spiders as well as flies and other insects.

12 inches
(30 cm)

Height it can reach in one jump

Leap

The jaws of the archerfish play a vital role in the hunt.

The pectoral fins power its leap.

▼ African Butterfly Fish

In the water the tail powers its ascent to the surface.

The pectoral fins serve as wings.

▼ Hatchetfish

Large, well-focused eyes for effective hunting

2.75 inches (7 cm)
Length of the hatchetfish

Assortment of Shapes

Most fish have a typical streamlined shape, like salmon or trout. Other species have developed widely varying characteristics as *adaptations* to their environment or diet. The longnose hawkfish's snout helps it eat *invertebrates* on the seabed. The stiff, slender body of the longhorn cowfish causes it to swim slowly and clumsily. And the clown knifefish has a flattened, knifelike body that enables it to move more easily through the water.

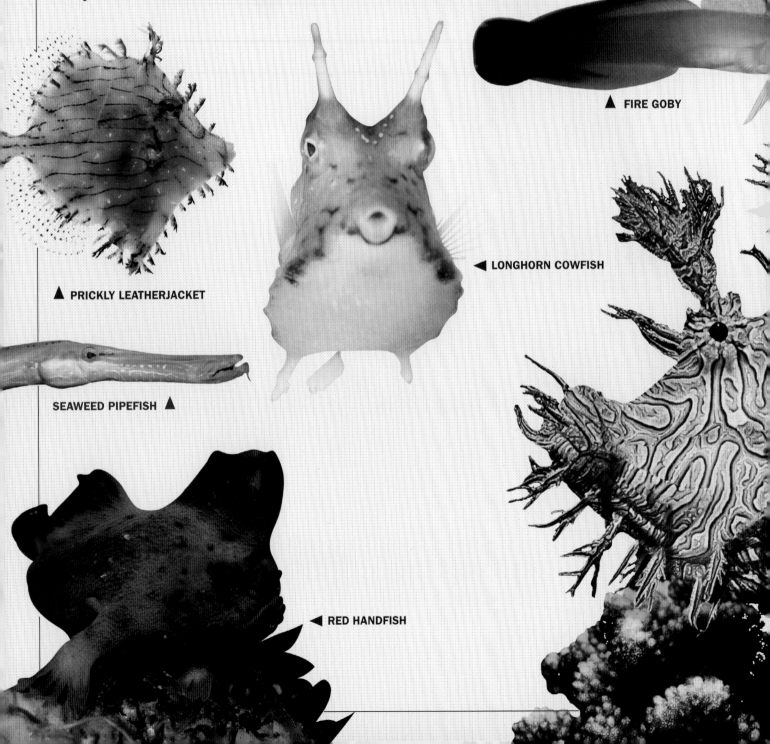

▲ FIRE GOBY

◄ LONGHORN COWFISH

▲ PRICKLY LEATHERJACKET

SEAWEED PIPEFISH ▲

◄ RED HANDFISH

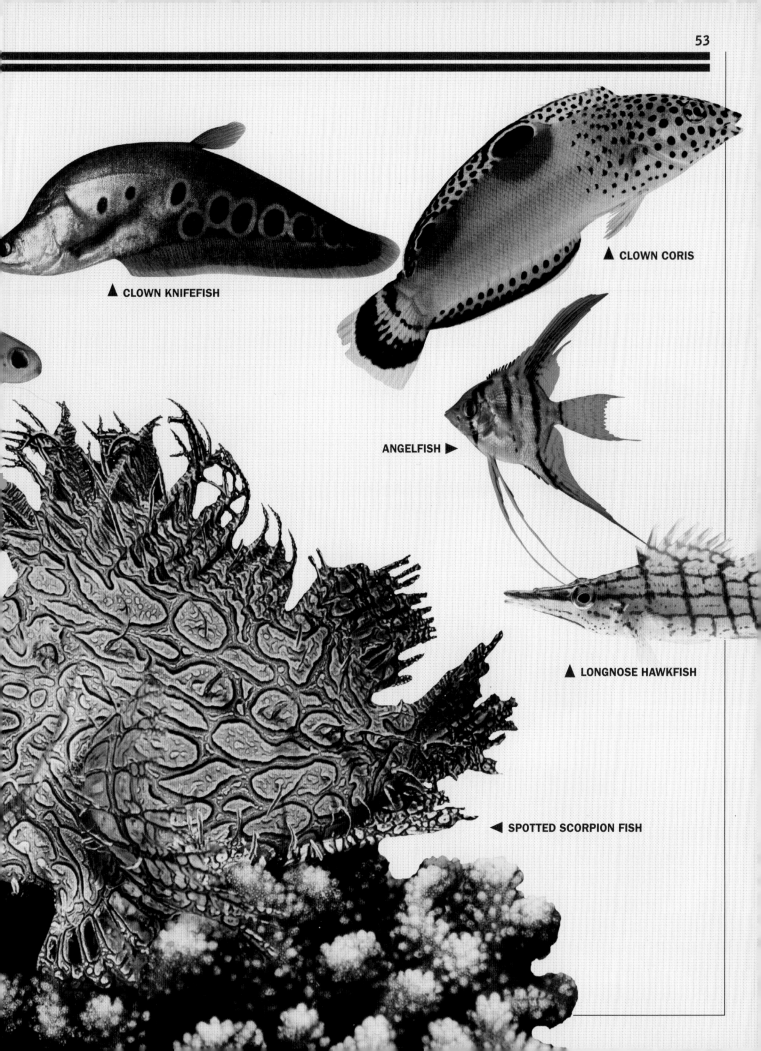

▲ CLOWN KNIFEFISH

▲ CLOWN CORIS

ANGELFISH ▶

▲ LONGNOSE HAWKFISH

◀ SPOTTED SCORPION FISH

Wonders of Color

Fish use color to communicate with others of their *species*. They also use color in mating rituals and even to hide from their prey. A young emperor angelfish has blue and white spirals, but it develops its own appearance when it reaches maturity. This helps it to find a mate and define its territory. Today science is discovering how fish perceive differences of color and what sort of messages the colors convey.

EMPEROR ANGELFISH ▶

◀ SIAMESE FIGHTING FISH

▲ OCELLARIS CLOWNFISH

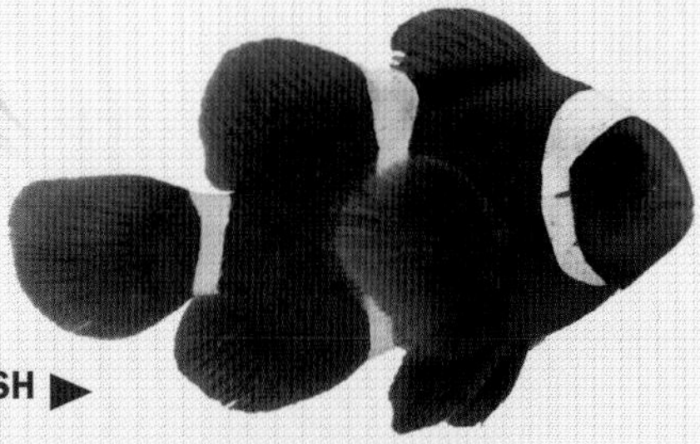

PERCULA CLOWNFISH ▶

◀ HUMPBACK GROUPER

▼ WRASSE

▲ CLOWN TRIGGERFISH

▲ GOLDFISH

▲ WHITETAIL DAMSELFISH

▲ HARLEQUIN TUSKFISH

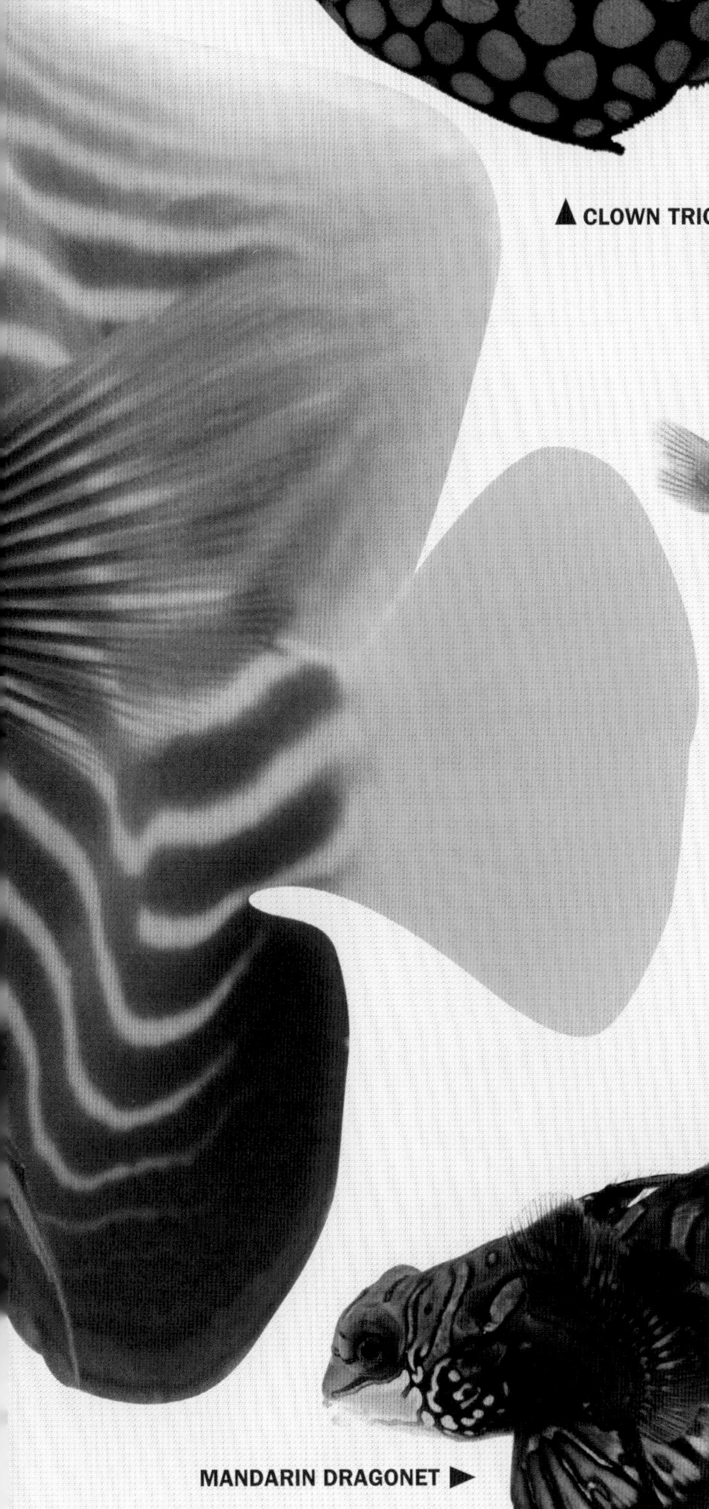

MANDARIN DRAGONET ▶

THREADFIN BUTTERFLY FISH ▶

Matters of Life and Death

To survive, most fish need *adaptations* to enable them to flee from their predators or to find food. The European plaice can lie on the ocean floor with its flat body. Its ivory color makes it almost invisible. The flying fish, on the other hand, developed *pectoral fins* to lift itself up over the surface of the water and flee its enemies.

European Plaice

Mouth

VENTRAL SIDE

EYES

GILLS

OPERCULUM

A FLATTENED FORM

Leafy Sea Dragon

CAMOUFLAGE

SEAWEED

Flying Fish

1 Escape

2 Takeoff

3 Gliding

They reach heights of up to 19 feet (6 m).

Flying fish measure from 7 to 18 inches (18 to 45 cm) long.

These fish cover distances of up to 160 feet (50 m) in the air.

ANATOMY

SPOTS

FIN

CAUDAL FIN

Scorpion Fish

Danger in the Water

There are poisonous fish in all the seas in the world. The toxic substances they produce are usually not meant for threatening humans but for defending themselves from larger aquatic *predators*. Although some species of puffer fish have poisonous flesh, in Japan they are considered a delicacy when properly prepared.

A Swimming Fortress

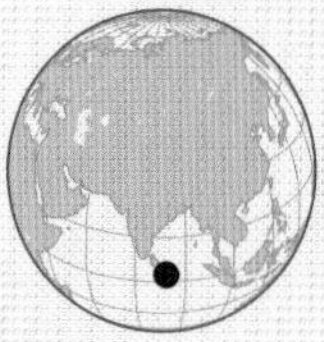

RED LIONFISH

Habitat	Indian and Pacific oceans, Sri Lanka
Largest size	15 inches (38 cm)
Family	Scorpaenidae

Like a Peacock

TWO PECTORAL SPINES

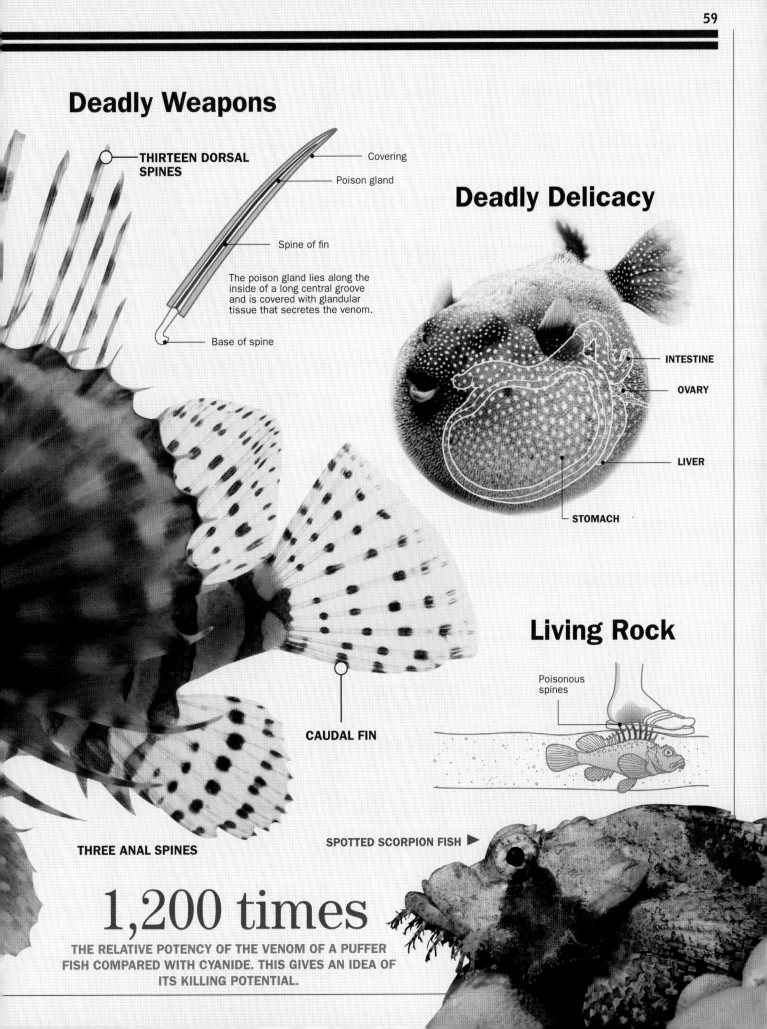

Deadly Weapons

THIRTEEN DORSAL SPINES

Covering

Poison gland

Spine of fin

The poison gland lies along the inside of a long central groove and is covered with glandular tissue that secretes the venom.

Base of spine

Deadly Delicacy

INTESTINE

OVARY

LIVER

STOMACH

Living Rock

Poisonous spines

CAUDAL FIN

THREE ANAL SPINES

SPOTTED SCORPION FISH ▶

1,200 times

THE RELATIVE POTENCY OF THE VENOM OF A PUFFER FISH COMPARED WITH CYANIDE. THIS GIVES AN IDEA OF ITS KILLING POTENTIAL.

The Best Disguise

To face their enemies, fish have developed a number of strategies to enable them to survive. Some of these are escaping, hiding in the ocean bed, or stirring up sand to avoid being seen. Other species have poison, and some can inflate and raise barbs or spines to discourage predators. In the oceans' depths are fish that have luminous organs that blind the enemy.

Spot-Fin Porcupine Fish

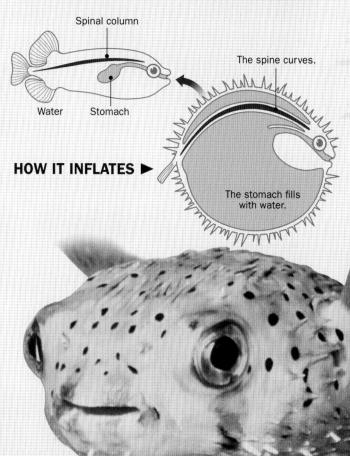

Spinal column

Water   Stomach

The spine curves.

HOW IT INFLATES ▶

The stomach fills with water.

SELF-DEFENSE ▲

AT REST ▲

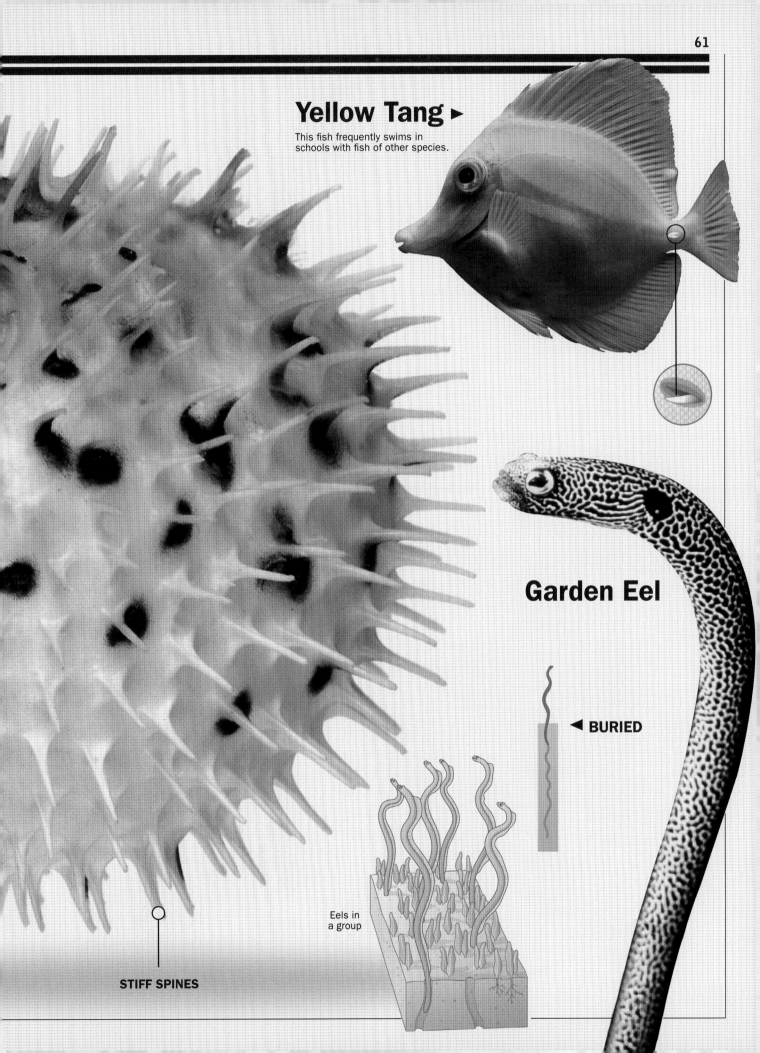

Yellow Tang ▶

This fish frequently swims in schools with fish of other species.

Garden Eel

◀ BURIED

Eels in a group

STIFF SPINES

Kings of Darkness

In depths below 8,200 feet (2,500 m), where barely any light penetrates, live rare species known as abyssal fish. In this environment, life is possible near hydrothermal vents in the seafloor that warm the nearby waters. In spite of this natural warmth, in many areas the temperature never rises above 36° F (2° C). At this depth fish have peculiar shapes, with large heads and strong teeth for eating other fish, since no vegetation can grow there. To attract their prey, many have "lure" organs made of photophores that shine in the darkness. They also are usually black or dark brown for purposes of camouflage.

LANTERN
Like most abyssal fish, it has a lure organ.

EYES FOR SEEING IN DIM LIGHT

Ray of light

FILAMENTS
cover its entire body for protection.

Dragonfish

FUMAROLE

36°F (2°C)

TEMPERATURE OF WATER HEATED BY FUMAROLES

CHIN APPENDAGE

Fangtooth Viperfish

SKIN

GLOWING LURE

DIMENSIONS

4 inches (10 cm)

Weight
10.6 ounces
(300 g)

Illuminated Netdevil

KILLER JAWS

GLOWING LURE

Atlantic Football

CHIN APPENDAGE

TAIL AND FINS

BODY

Sea Snakes

Eels are an order of ray-finned fish with distinctively snakelike shapes. There are about 600 species of true eels, including morays, congers, and snake eels. Eels come in a wide variety of colors and patterns, ranging from solid gray to mottled yellow. Their bodies lack *scales* and are covered with a protective mucous membrane. One of the most striking eels is the green moray, which lives in the Caribbean Sea and hides in *coral reefs* awaiting its prey. Although it is not poisonous, it is feared by divers because its bite can inflict grave wounds.

GREEN MORAY

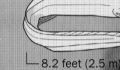

8.2 feet (2.5 m)

Habitat	Caribbean Sea
Depth	25-200 feet (8-60 m)
Weight	64 pounds (29 kg)

Green Moray ▶

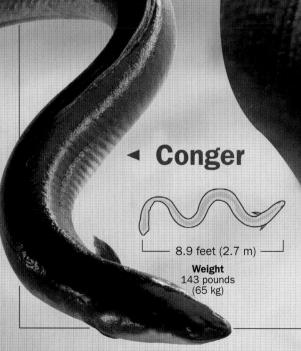

◀ **Conger**

8.9 feet (2.7 m)

Weight
143 pounds
(65 kg)

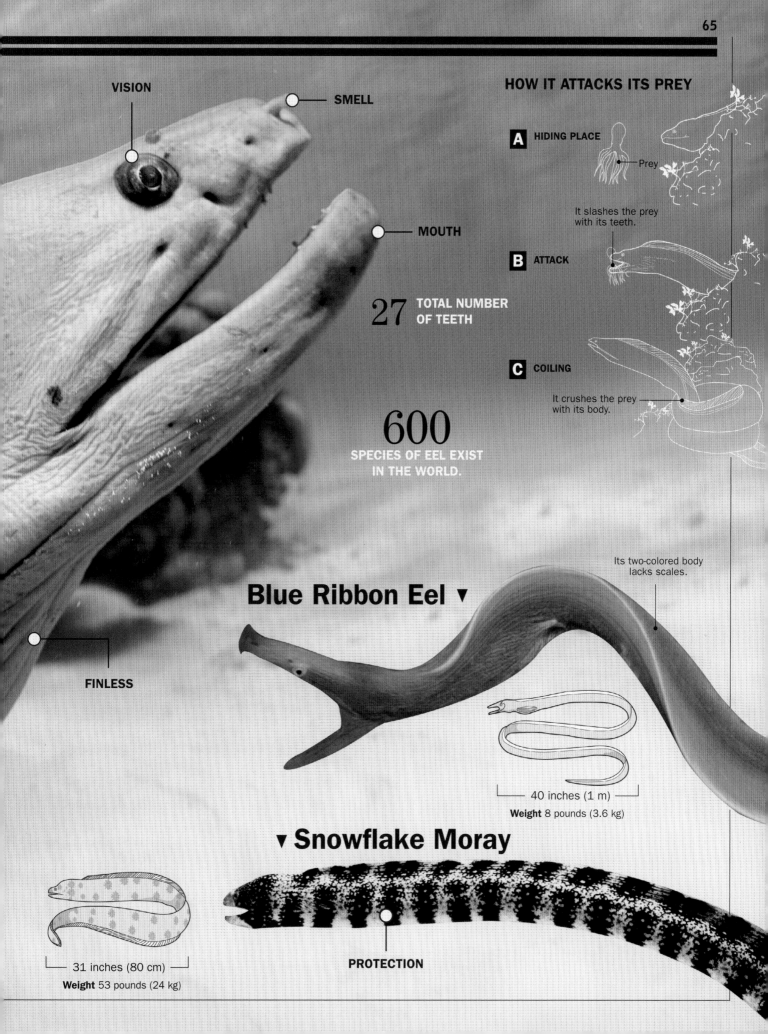

VISION

SMELL

HOW IT ATTACKS ITS PREY

A HIDING PLACE

Prey

It slashes the prey
with its teeth.

B ATTACK

MOUTH

27 **TOTAL NUMBER
OF TEETH**

C COILING

It crushes the prey
with its body.

600
**SPECIES OF EEL EXIST
IN THE WORLD.**

Its two-colored body
lacks scales.

Blue Ribbon Eel ▼

FINLESS

40 inches (1 m)
Weight 8 pounds (3.6 kg)

▼ Snowflake Moray

31 inches (80 cm)
Weight 53 pounds (24 kg)

PROTECTION

Out of the Water

Some *species* of fish can breathe and live out of the water. They include the mudskippers in southeast Asia, which can stay on muddy flats and even climb trees. To breathe, they need only their skin to stay moist, thanks to the function of certain cells in their skin. A few other species still have rudimentary lungs like those of the first aquatic animals that colonized dry land.

Fish with Lungs

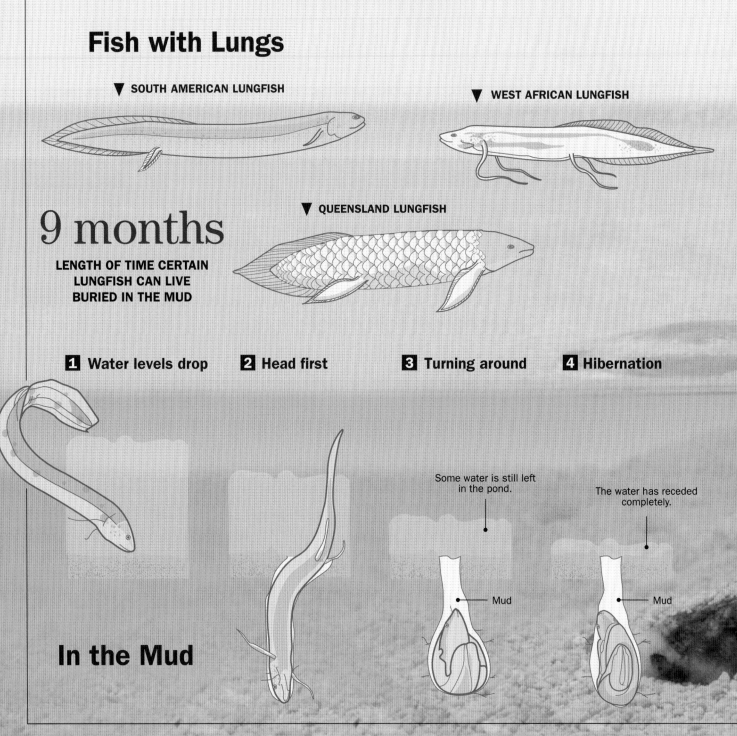

▼ SOUTH AMERICAN LUNGFISH

▼ WEST AFRICAN LUNGFISH

9 months
LENGTH OF TIME CERTAIN LUNGFISH CAN LIVE BURIED IN THE MUD

▼ QUEENSLAND LUNGFISH

1 Water levels drop   **2** Head first   **3** Turning around   **4** Hibernation

Some water is still left in the pond.

The water has receded completely.

Mud

Mud

In the Mud

EYES

WATER RESERVES

GILLS

Atlantic Mudskippers

MOUTH
AND THROAT

VENTRAL DISK

SKIN

FINS

MUSCULATURE

Fossils
**LUNGFISH HAVE NOT EVOLVED IN
250 MILLION YEARS.**

MUDSKIPPER

Habitat	Indian Ocean and the Pacific coasts of Asia
Family	Gobidae
Length	6 inches (15 cm)

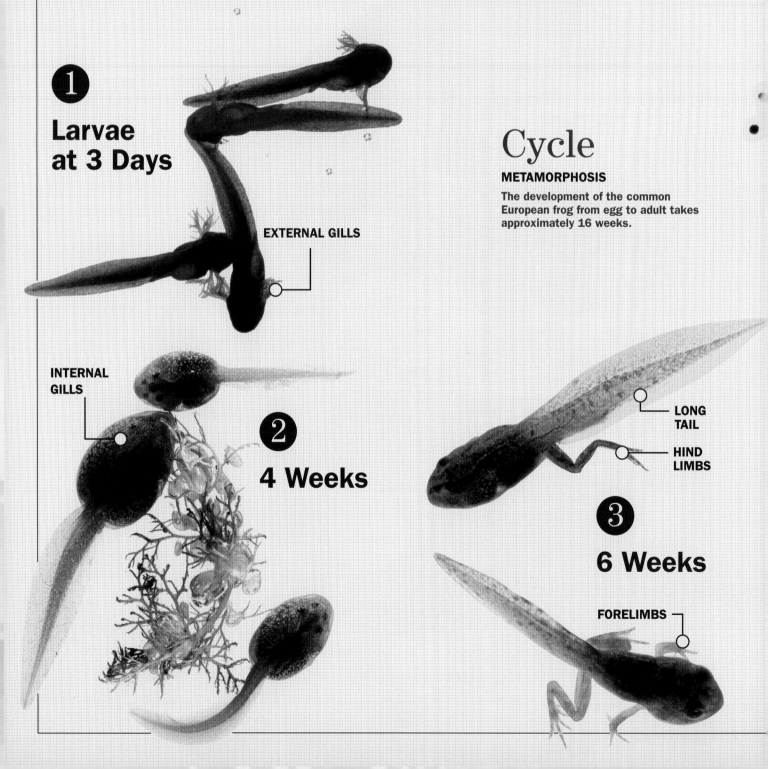

Metamorphosis

Metamorphosis is the process of transformation experienced by frogs, starting with the egg and ending at the adult stage. When they leave the egg, *amphibians* have a *larval* form. They then undergo very important changes in their anatomy, diet, and lifestyle, slowly mutating from their first stage, which is completely aquatic, until they transform into animals adapted to life on land.

1

Larvae at 3 Days

EXTERNAL GILLS

Cycle

METAMORPHOSIS

The development of the common European frog from egg to adult takes approximately 16 weeks.

INTERNAL GILLS

2

4 Weeks

LONG TAIL

HIND LIMBS

3

6 Weeks

FORELIMBS

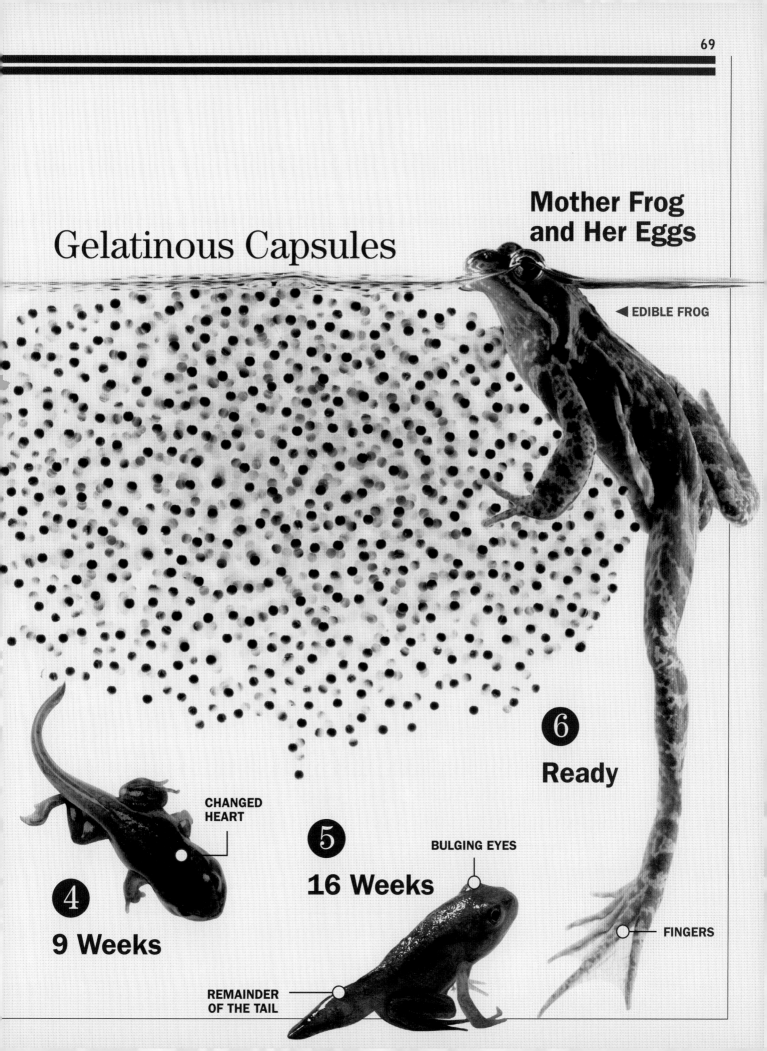

Gelatinous Capsules

Mother Frog and Her Eggs

◀ EDIBLE FROG

6
Ready

FINGERS

4
CHANGED HEART

9 Weeks

5
16 Weeks

BULGING EYES

REMAINDER OF THE TAIL

Turtles in the Water!

Sea turtles have had to _____ parts of their bodies to an aquatic environment. Their front legs propel them through the water, and their hind legs serve as rudders for steering. Their shells are highly streamlined. They can spend up to several hours submerged in the water, since they have a dual respiratory system. They lay eggs but make their nests on solid ground, and they have an interesting system for choosing the spot where their young will be born—they return to the same spot where they, themselves, were born.

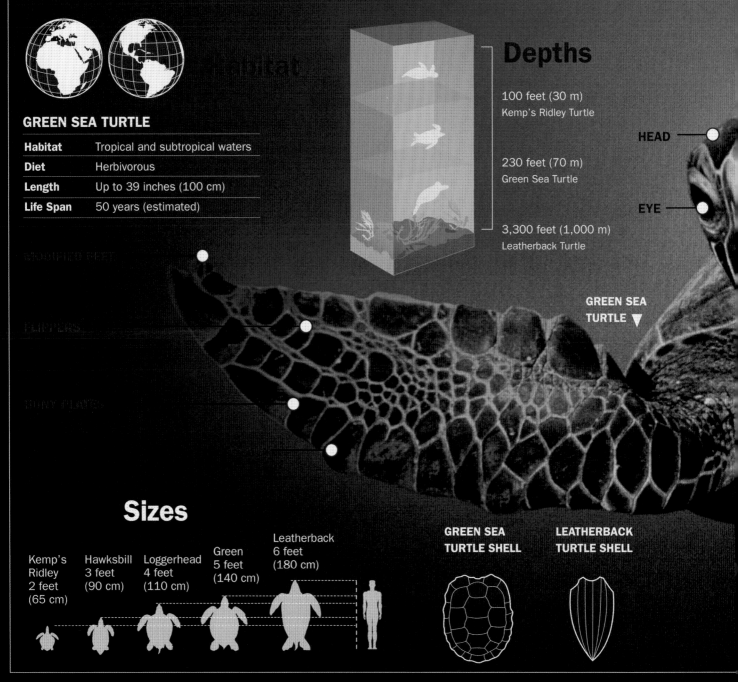

Habitat

GREEN SEA TURTLE

Habitat	Tropical and subtropical waters
Diet	Herbivorous
Length	Up to 39 inches (100 cm)
Life Span	50 years (estimated)

MODIFIED FEET

FLIPPERS

HIND FEET

Depths

100 feet (30 m)
Kemp's Ridley Turtle

230 feet (70 m)
Green Sea Turtle

3,300 feet (1,000 m)
Leatherback Turtle

HEAD

EYE

GREEN SEA
TURTLE ▼

Sizes

Kemp's
Ridley
2 feet
(65 cm)

Hawksbill
3 feet
(90 cm)

Loggerhead
4 feet
(110 cm)

Green
5 feet
(140 cm)

Leatherback
6 feet
(180 cm)

**GREEN SEA
TURTLE SHELL**

**LEATHERBACK
TURTLE SHELL**

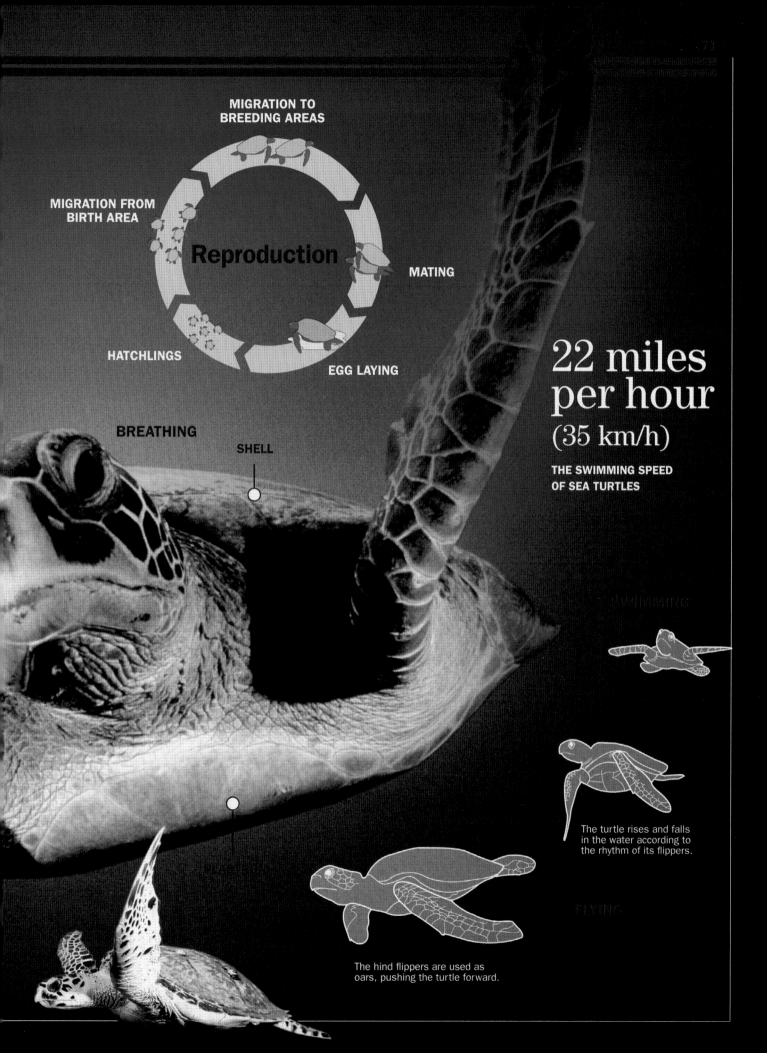

MIGRATION TO BREEDING AREAS

MIGRATION FROM BIRTH AREA

Reproduction

MATING

HATCHLINGS

EGG LAYING

BREATHING

SHELL

22 miles per hour
(35 km/h)

THE SWIMMING SPEED OF SEA TURTLES

The turtle rises and falls in the water according to the rhythm of its flippers.

The hind flippers are used as oars, pushing the turtle forward.

Marine Iguana

The marine iguana is the only *species* of iguana in the world that spends most of its time in the water. This reptile lives on the rocky coasts of the Galapagos Islands and feeds on seaweed and *algae*. It can stay underwater for 45 minutes and dive approximately 50 feet (15 m) deep. This unique, slow-swimming creature gathers seaweed to eat at low tide or dives for food.

A Galapagos Native

SCALY BACK

LEGS

MARINE IGUANA

Habitat	Semi-aquatic
Length	20-40 inches (50-100 cm)
Range	Galapagos Islands

40 inches (1 m)
Weight 24 pounds (11 kg)

Galapagos

Pinta

Roca Redonda

Marchena   Genovesa

Equator 0°

Santiago Bartolomé

Seymour

Rábida   Baltra

Fernandina   Santa Cruz   San Cristóbal

Pinzón

Santa Fe   1°

GALAPAGOS ISLANDS

Isabela

Española

Floreana
(Isla Santa María)

91°   90°

45 MINUTES UNDERWATER WITHOUT AIR
is the maximum amount of time that a marine iguana
can stay submerged while looking for food.

Swimming Style

SPINES

Its tail is thick
and flat.

Wavelike movements of
its body propel it forward.

Its legs are bent
to the side.

SALT

SEAWEED

CLAWS

Feeding Habits

Out of the water
They sun themselves on
the coast, where their
colonies live.

Intermediate Zone
They walk or dive for
food, depending on the
tide level.

HIGH TIDE
12 hours

Sea Level

Seaweed

LOW TIDE
12 hours

Diving Zone
Seaweed is abundant
but can only be reached
by diving.

The Language of Water

Dolphins are sophisticated communicators. They click with their mandibles when in trouble and whistle repeatedly when afraid or excited. During courtship and mating, they touch and caress. They also communicate through visual signals—such as leaping—to show that food is close by.

HAVING FUN

Common Name	Bottlenose dolphin
Family	Delphinidae
Adult Weight	330 to 1,400 pounds (150 to 650 kg)
Longevity	30 to 40 years

7 to 13 feet (2-4 m)

They reach
22 mph (35 km/h)

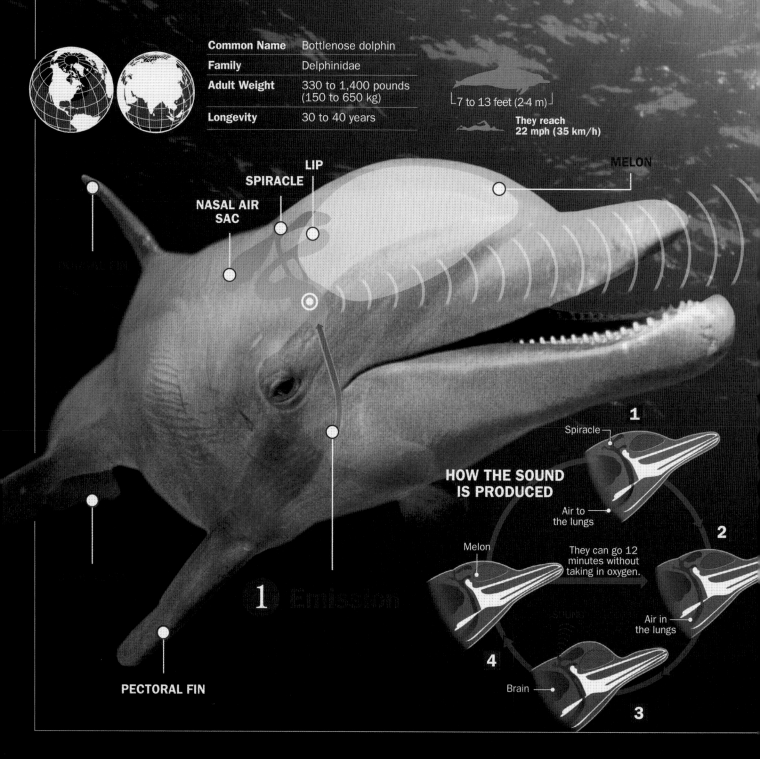

LIP

SPIRACLE

NASAL AIR
SAC

MELON

DORSAL FIN

1 Emission

PECTORAL FIN

**HOW THE SOUND
IS PRODUCED**

1
Spiracle

Air to
the lungs

Melon

They can go 12
minutes without
taking in oxygen.

2

Air in
the lungs

4

Brain

3

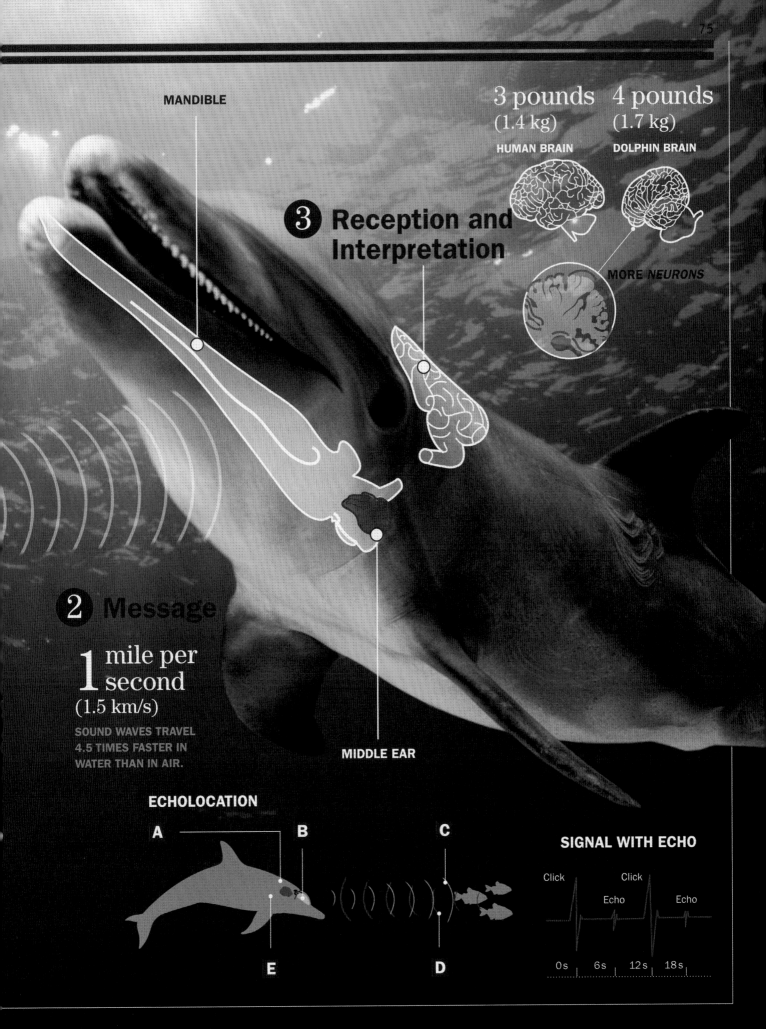

MANDIBLE

3 Reception and Interpretation

3 pounds
(1.4 kg)

4 pounds
(1.7 kg)

HUMAN BRAIN

DOLPHIN BRAIN

MORE *NEURONS*

2 Message

1 mile per second
(1.5 km/s)

SOUND WAVES TRAVEL
4.5 TIMES FASTER IN
WATER THAN IN AIR.

MIDDLE EAR

ECHOLOCATION

A

B

C

E

D

SIGNAL WITH ECHO

Click

Click

Echo

Echo

0s   6s   12s   18s

Record Breath-Holders

Sperm whales are unique animals whose *species* is remarkable for many reasons. They have the ability to dive to a maximum depth of 9,800 feet (3,000 m) and remain underwater without oxygen for up to two hours. They are able to do this because they can decrease their heart rate, store and use air in the muscles, and prioritize the delivery of oxygen to certain vital organs such as the heart and lungs. They are the largest whales with teeth, which are found only on the lower mandible.

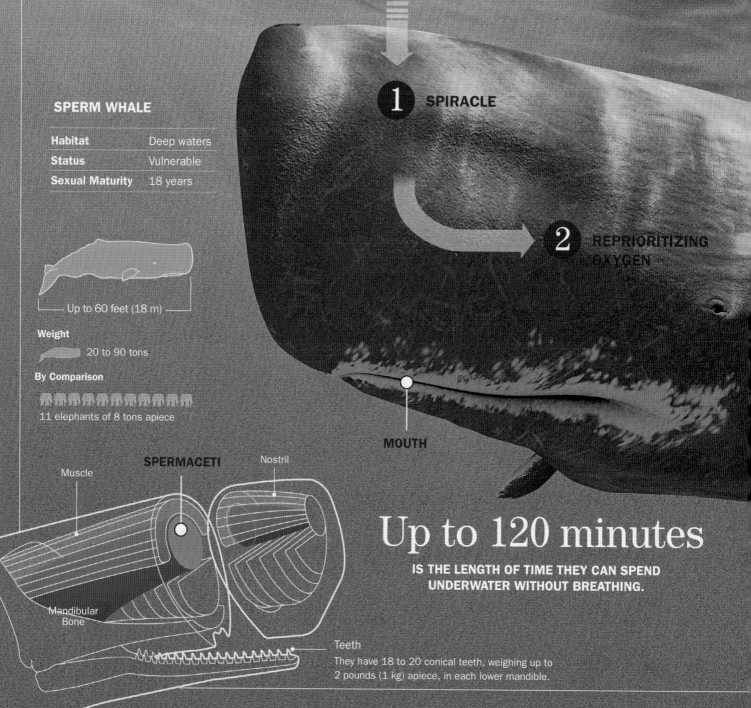

SPERM WHALE

Habitat	Deep waters
Status	Vulnerable
Sexual Maturity	18 years

Up to 60 feet (18 m)

Weight

20 to 90 tons

By Comparison

11 elephants of 8 tons apiece

1 SPIRACLE

2 REPRIORITIZING OXYGEN

MOUTH

SPERMACETI

Muscle

Nostril

Mandibular Bone

Teeth
They have 18 to 20 conical teeth, weighing up to 2 pounds (1 kg) apiece, in each lower mandible.

Up to 120 minutes

IS THE LENGTH OF TIME THEY CAN SPEND UNDERWATER WITHOUT BREATHING.

Adaptation in Respiration

ON THE SURFACE

Blowhole remains open, allowing the whales to breathe as much oxygen as they can before diving.

WHEN THEY DIVE

Powerful muscles tightly close the opening of the blowhole, keeping water from entering.

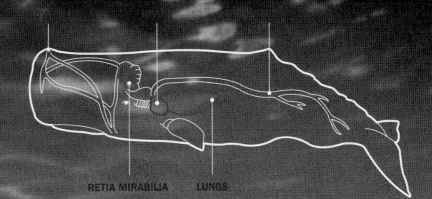

RETIA MIRABILIA   LUNGS

③ BRADYCARDIA

Dive

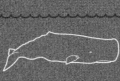

0 FEET (0 M)
ON THE SURFACE

+ 3,300 FEET
(1,000 M)
90 MINUTES

0 FEET (0 M)
ON THE SURFACE

Making Use of Oxygen

15%

**AMOUNT OF AIR
REPLACED IN ONE BREATH**

85%

**AMOUNT OF AIR
REPLACED IN ONE BREATH**

Habitat, Tastes, and Preferences

The oceans cover 70 percent of the Earth's surface. That is where life began on this planet and where the most primitive *species* live side by side with the most highly evolved ones. This abundance of species is due in part to the wide variety of environments found in the ocean. As one descends in depth, the water's temperature decreases, as does the amount of light. These factors determine different *ecosystems*, feeding regimes, and *adaptation* strategies among a wide variety of fish species.

Reserve of Life

REEFS ▲

0-650 feet
(0-200 m)
EPIPELAGIC ZONE

490 feet
(150 m)

FLYING FISH

TRUMPET FISH

CLOWNFISH

SWORDFISH

HAMMERHEAD
SHARK

MANTA RAY

SNAPPER

SERGEANT FISH

BLUE
ANGELFISH

MORAY EEL

STRIPED
PERCH

BARRACUDA

OCEAN SUNFISH

TIGER
SHARK

PUFFER
FISH

30 FEET (9 M)
Divers without
special equipment

50 FEET (15 M)
Pearl divers

160 FEET (50 M)
Scuba divers

**ABUNDANT
PLANKTON**
at this level

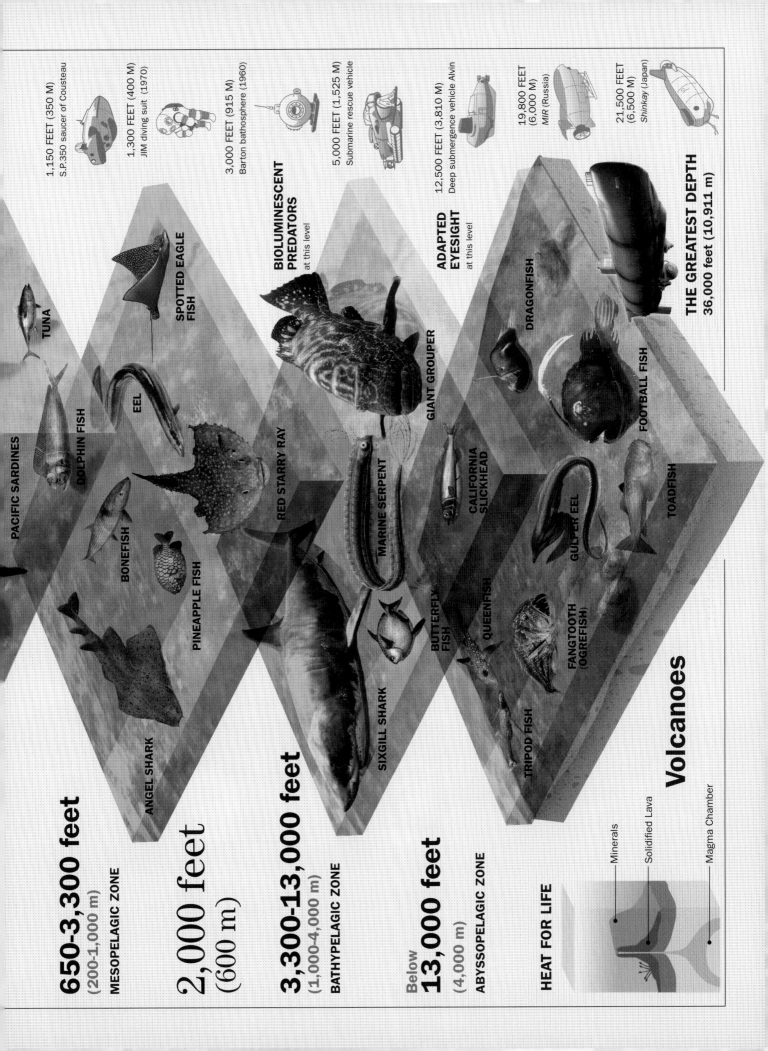

1,150 FEET (350 M)
S.P.350 saucer of Cousteau

1,300 FEET (400 M)
JIM diving suit (1970)

3,000 FEET (915 M)
Barton bathosphere (1960)

5,000 FEET (1,525 M)
Submarine rescue vehicle

12,500 FEET (3,810 M)
Deep submergence vehicle Alvin

19,800 FEET
(6,000 M)
MIR (Russia)

21,500 FEET
(6,500 M)
Shinkay (Japan)

TUNA

SPOTTED EAGLE FISH

EEL

DOLPHIN FISH

PACIFIC SARDINES

BONEFISH

PINEAPPLE FISH

ANGEL SHARK

RED STARRY RAY

BIOLUMINESCENT PREDATORS at this level

GIANT GROUPER

MARINE SERPENT

CALIFORNIA SLICKHEAD

ADAPTED EYESIGHT at this level

DRAGONFISH

FOOTBALL FISH

THE GREATEST DEPTH
36,000 feet (10,911 m)

GULPER EEL

TOADFISH

SIXGILL SHARK

BUTTERFLY FISH

QUEENFISH

FANGTOOTH (OGREFISH)

TRIPOD FISH

650-3,300 feet
(200-1,000 m)

MESOPELAGIC ZONE

2,000 feet
(600 m)

3,300-13,000 feet
(1,000-4,000 m)

BATHYPELAGIC ZONE

Below
13,000 feet
(4,000 m)

ABYSSOPELAGIC ZONE

HEAT FOR LIFE

Volcanoes

Minerals

Solidified Lava

Magma Chamber

Endangered Species

Indiscriminate hunting, overfishing, and pollution of the oceans have pushed many species to the brink of extinction. Sharks and rays are among the first marine life-forms to be systematically studied, and 20 percent of their 547 species are in danger of disappearing. Slow-growing species are especially susceptible to excessive fishing.

HUMPHEAD WRASSE ►

Status	Endangered
Cause	Pollution
Range	Pacific and Indian oceans

ANGEL SHARK

Status	Critically endangered
Cause	Overfishing
Range	Mediterranean Sea and Black Sea

COMMON SKATE

Status	Vulnerable
Cause	Overfishing
Range	Eastern Atlantic

WHALE SHARK

Status	Endangered
Cause	Indiscriminate fishing
Range	Warm seas

YELLOWCROWNED BUTTERFLY FISH

Status	Vulnerable
Cause	Pollution
Range	Guam

PYGMY SEAHORSE

Status	Endangered
Cause	Pollution
Range	Caribbean Sea

PERSIAN STURGEON

Status	Endangered
Cause	Overfishing
Range	Caspian Sea